LIFE AND LITERATURE

in the Roman Republic

"This book grew out of an effort to visualize a few of the early Roman writers in their response to their own environment. My generation was brought up to look upon the Roman as a kind of double-faced herm. In the senate-house, in the Forum, in the fields of jurisprudence and administration, the Roman revealed daring, versatility, imagination, and even philosophical penetration, whereas in literary expression, we were told, he was utterly imitative. The picture was not very convincing. Have we misread the modern connotations of the term 'imitation'? Have we neglected to penetrate the fog of concealing centuries into the active, pulsating life of Roman men and women, and pursued instead the easier task of detecting parallels?" —TENNEY FRANK

TENNEY FRANK

LIFE

AND

LITERATURE

IN THE ROMAN REPUBLIC

UNIVERSITY OF CALIFORNIA PRESS

Berkeley, Los Angeles, London   1971

University of California Press
Berkeley and Los Angeles, California
University of California Press, Ltd.
London, England

Originally published as Volume Seven of the
Sather Classical Lectures

Sixth printing, 1971
ISBN: 0-520-00428-0

PRINTED IN THE UNITED STATES OF AMERICA

CONTENTS

CHAPTER I

INTRODUCTION: SOCIAL FORCES

The story of intellectual pioneering, visualized with difficulty, has not the thrill of a Marco Polo diary, but to the intelligent it has a deeper fascination. Our records are, however, very brief, spanning a few thousand out of many hundred thousand years. What we can review is a small fraction of the whole story. If the human race is more than 300,000 years old, man's artistic literature is less than 3000: our segment of sure knowledge is less than one per cent of the amazing tale. If the biologist is willing to pry into the strata of a hundred million years to trace the evolution of plant and animal life, it is hardly conceivable that the humanist should disregard any part of our pitifully meager record of spiritual endeavor. This is my excuse for inviting attention to the first efforts of the Romans to express themselves in literary form.

In attempting to tell a part of this story I have chosen to notice especially how the writers of the period responded to their environment, because this aspect of the theme has been somewhat neglected in recent studies of Roman literature. This is of course not a novel method of approach. Taine, for instance, drove the hobby of environmental determinism at a gallop that ought to satisfy the most optimistic behaviorist, and his immediate followers never checked the rein. The method has since had its more deliberate devotees. English classicists in particular, who have usually studied history and literature together, have generally kept a sane and fruitful coordination of men and their milieu. During the last three decades, however, there has been so strong a trend toward deep and narrow specialization in our own universities that here the literary historian has been tempted to neglect social, political, and artistic history with unfortunate results. For instance, the scholar who studies classical prose forms has often kept his eye so intent upon the accumulation of rhetorical rules from Gorgias to Cicero that he has given us a history of a futile scholastic mechanism and not of an ever-vitalized prose which in fact re-created its appropriate medium with every new generation. The scholastic critics of the Roman lyric are sometimes so intent upon tracing external conventions through the centuries that they miss the soul of the poetry that assumes temporarily the mold of the convention. The same is true of all the literary forms. "Sources and influences," as traceable in words, phrases, and literary customs, things which after all seldom explain creative inspiration, are rather attractive game to men of good verbal memories and are likely to entice them away from the larger work of penetrating comprehension. Beethovan's fifth symphony receives little illumination from program notes pedantically informing us that the "fate motif" is a borrowed phrase.

Here and there a reaction against an exaggerated reiteration of literary influences has driven critics into the school of those who prefer to approach literature as a "pure" art. Such critics seem to justify their doctrine when they confine their analysis to the more transcendental passages of Shakespeare or Keats, Catullus or Sophocles. When dealing, however, with Dante, Goethe, Vergil, Milton, and in fact with most poets of generous social sympathies, they give a very inadequate account of the poetic product. Modern aesthetics have been teaching us how warm with subjective interpretation is that thing we call beauty. Apparently there is no such thing, even in poetry, as pure, objective, absolute art uniformly sustained. In fact no school of criticism has as yet formulated a doctrine wide enough to compass the broad ranges of artistic creation, nor need we expect an adequate science of aesthetics unless psychology can become scientific.

The protest on the part of one vociferous school of humanists that literary criticism must disregard history and biography is beside the mark so long as our prying minds insist on prying. Contemporaneous literature, of course, deserves first of all to be approached with the aesthetic perceptions all alert, and since the reader lives in the same world as the writer the scant exegesis that may be necessary can be absorbed unconsciously from the text itself. But any great literature of the far past becomes to us, in so far as we are normal humans, something besides art. It is also a body of documents that anyone at all interested in the progress of art, of ideas, or of society in any of its groupings, may find very precious, and he will persist in using it as documentary despite all the protests of jealous literary criticism. For Greece and Rome our documents are none too abundant in any case. It is a very petty humanism that dares insist that no one may touch Vergil or Spenser except and only for aesthetic delight and judgments. It is of course wholly legitimate to read Dante for his haunting lines and his stupendous imagery, but many of us insist on the added privilege of transporting ourselves into his mysterious world of strange ideas if only to read him as did his contemporaries. The true humanist in any case is interested in more than artistic expression, and the humanist who deals with remote literature must be, perforce.

It is of course only fair to say that in calling attention to milieu we would not deny that the innate endowment of each author is and must be considered the prime factor in creative work, while admitting that it may be the most elusive item to analyze. Modern biology insists upon the reality of inheritance, though it also warns us that this inheritance is so complex that it has hitherto escaped analysis and predetermination. We all admit that the study of social or literary atmosphere or of individual training will not explain the passionate force of Catullus, the voluble humor of Plautus, or Cicero's ear for harmony of sound. However, like Horace in his *Ars Poetica*, we can do little but admit the facts, recognize the qualities, and proceed to the study of the provocative stimuli.

Moreover, there are special reasons for attempting to place Roman writers in their environment. One is that the evidence regarding the status of Roman society is so scant and so scattered that the casual reader cannot be expected to have a correct understanding of it, and even the specialist is apt to neglect the severe task of reconstructing the social staging. As a result the literary history of the classics too often leaves us with the incorrect feeling that we have there only cold impersonal conventions.

Another is that the milieu is so different from our own that the imagination when left unguarded is in danger of modernizing ancient life and ancient expression to such an extent as to distort both scenery and actors. This is not questioning the fact that the Greeks and Romans were precisely like us. Their bodies had the same capacities, needs, and passions as ours, their senses received impressions as ours, their brains met problems by the same logical processes as ours, despite the amusing claim of the pragmatists that they are just now teaching the true art of "operational thinking." In these respects the advanced races seem to have reached full development very far back in prehistoric times, many millenia before Homer. The pseudo-anthropology which a few years ago assumed that the study of Hottentot psychology might be useful to the student of Plato joked itself off the stage. The critics who tried to persuade us that the romantic sentiment came into being less than a thousand years ago seem equally ludicrous now. We need not repeat the egregious error of Spengler in confounding mental capacities with temporary conventions of expression that tried to respond to environmental need.

But while granting that human nature was then what it is now, it is important to comprehend the diversity of the customs, fashions, traditions, conventions, and social needs which evoked an appropriate artistic expression that consequently differs from our own. Love and hate doubtless stirred very similar physical sensations in Catullus, in Dante, and in Tennyson, but the words which these three poets used to express those emotions in verses published for their own readers have very different connotations, because the conventions of their respective periods called for a different series of suppressions and revelations. None of the three can be translated directly into the language of any of the others without evoking erroneous impressions. The pagan directness of Catullus' lines, the Platonic connotations of the *Nuova Vita*, the Christian romanticism of Tennyson are worlds apart, not because the human being changes but because his environment does. The devotees of nudity who know only the idiom of their own day may accuse Thackeray of hypocrisy because they have not learned to translate him; but that is not literary criticism. Those who miss in Latin poetry the delight in the outburst of spring-time song and color common in medieval poetry from north of the Alps have been prone to assume a temperamental lack in the classical poet, whereas the simple explanation may be that in the north spring brings a sense of release that is hardly realized in Latium where roses linger on till January when the new crocuses and windflowers start into blossom. The love of the sea was hardly to be expected till seafaring became fairly safe; the discovery of the compass has a place in the history of romanticism. The romantic enthusiasm for rugged mountain landscape could hardly arise in poets who knew only the placid hills of Italy and to whom the high Alps were known chiefly as the haunts of barbaric bandits.

Accurate interpretation of any author of the past, therefore, implies a complete migration into the time, the society, and the environment of that author. And herein lies the necessity of attempting the difficult task of placing the literary figures which we wish to discuss in their setting. In this first chapter, therefore, I shall attempt to sketch in outline the social changes that need to be kept in mind for the more detailed study of some of the writers of the Republican period.

Rome's beginnings in self-expression are not so fascinating as those of Greece. The Greeks somehow outstripped all competitors. In mental vigor, in imaginative creativeness, in sureness of taste, they seem to have reached a point 2500 years ago that the more advanced of modern racial groups are still hoping to attain. The sudden flowering of literature as soon as the capacities of the recording art were realized can only be comprehended on the assumption that singing, reciting, narrating, and disputing had proceeded for ages among their ancestors before the alphabet came into use. One may readily imagine that some of the ancestors of the Greeks discussed the "idea of good" around the cavern fire thousands of years before Plato. Brains of that capacity do not suddenly pullulate. Language as supple and rich as Homer's presupposes ages of keen perceiving and precise talking. But what conclusions those cavemen philosophers reached vanished with the smoke of the hearth fire because no man recorded them. The tale of what the Greek imagination accomplished after it could operate on accumulated records is one the like of which we shall probably never hear again.

Rome's story is less startling, must perforce be, since like ours, it was subsequent. One does not discover the North Pole or Betelgeuse twice. When the Romans reached the stage of self-consciousness, when they felt the desire to express themselves they found in well-nigh perfect mold the natural forms of expression, developed with sure taste by the Greeks out of song, dance, march-hymn, devotional prayer, dirge, entertaining narrative, or mimic representation. Song, drama, and dialogue are inevitable forms, given human nature, and the forms were at hand and were taken over by the Latins, as they were once more by the Italians at the end of medieval days, when learning disclosed the worth of Rome's literature.

Rome's literature made generous use of that of Greece. How much time it saved by entering into such an inheritance we do not know. How much vigor and realism it lost by yielding to the overwhelming persuasion of Greek writers we cannot say. Dante and Petrarch drank from Latin to the point of quickening creation, too many others to the point of dazed intoxication. There were times when the Latin authors also drank too deeply. But what was important was that just when the first contact was made the Romans had reached the mental maturity and developed the capacity to comprehend and use. There were many other peoples of the same period on whom Greek culture was wholly lost because they were incapable of appreciating it. The Phrygians, Cappadocians, Paphlagonians, Galatians, Armenians, half a dozen Thracian tribes, Syrians, Egyptians, Sicilians, Carthaginians, Oscans, Umbrians, Etruscans, Celts, Iberians, and a score of other tribes contemporaneous with the Romans, and in outward appearances of about the same stage of culture, came into direct contact with the Greeks, some for a much longer period and more intimately than the Latins, and yet they remained unfruitful in literary production. The Romans in fact were the only folk of the scores of neighbors of Greece that as a nation assimilated and worthily carried on the new-found culture.

What were the Romans like at that time—at the beginning of contact with the older Greeks in the middle of the third century B.C.? They were a small group of a few hundred thousand souls, one group of several that had emerged from barbarous central Europe and pushed their way into Italy in search for land, and they had long plodded on in silence at the dull task of making the soil provide food. For a while they had been subdued by the Etruscans, but taught by their conquerors to use arms in strong masses, they had applied this lesson by driving off their oppressors and re-establishing their old independent town meetings, returning again to the tilling of the soil. A prolific and puritanic folk with a strict social morality they outgrew their boundaries and began to expand. In the contests that resulted the Romans came off the victors. In organizing the adjacent tribes into a federal union they revealed a peculiar liberalism—unmatched anywhere among the barbarians of that day—by abstaining from the exaction of tribute; they also betrayed an imagination of high quality in the invention of cooperative leagues, and unusual capacity for legal logic in the shaping of municipal and civic forms. The inventiveness of the barbarian federation-builders of the last fifty years of the fourth century B.C. still commands the admiration of historians, even though all this work was done silently and with so little consciousness of its high quality that no one even thought of keeping a record of it. One does well not to call such a people unimaginative.

To be sure the Latins apparently had few myths or fairy tales, such as have arisen to aid literary effort in certain other regions. Perhaps a penchant for silent doing, a respect for logic and fact may be posited to explain this lack—though such an explanation merely begs the question. We still do not know what is meant by the inheritance of mental qualities. What "myth-making" is we also do not know.

In Greece, where myths grew everywhere to clothe poetic invention, we know at least that the migrant tribes had come in and inherited from the peoples of the Aegean world scores of anthropomorphic deities and heroes that in time aggregated into cycles of more or less related groups. Hittite heroes emerge as Greek gods and Cretan gods as Greek heroes. I do not mean to imply that accident explains all of Greek mythology, for the Greeks enjoyed tales and preserved them. But where the early contacts of the Greeks were fortunate, those of the Romans were not. The Romans on their arrival in central Italy knew no deities in personal form about which tales could gather, and when anthropomorphism came it was imposed by the Etruscans in connection with deities that were never wholly assimilated. The Romans stepped almost from primitive animism to sophistication, and presently to skepticism, and that experience denied them the poetic pabulum which has always been the most envigorating in early art.

Of primitive vocal expression in artistic form at Rome we know but little. It was as thoroughly obliterated by the onrush of Greek as was the native English epic and lyric by the Norman conquest; indeed more, since, not being written, it vanished, while the old English material survived at least in part in dusty archives. Old Romans later said they remembered having heard heroic ballads, and we believe them because the first Hellenizers found a native ballad meter (the Saturnian) which was so well established that they could use it for a translation of the Odyssey and for a native epic. Non-Romans like Livius and Naevius[1] would not have employed the Saturnian verse unless the popular ear had been accustomed to it and demanded it. There were also religious songs accompanied by dancing. A fragment of one of these songs in honor of Mars has survived in a late copy of an early ritual. In Greece a similar ritualistic song had the good fortune of being addressed to Dionysus, a more

[1] The tradition regarding early bards can be traced to the elder Cato. It is therefore not contaminated by the scholastic traditions which later vitiated the story of the drama.

genial deity, and it seems to have developed into the dithyramb and ultimately gave rise to the drama. On Mars, however, poetry was wasted.

Of a primitive drama we have a vigorous tradition. Simple comic farces were in existence in the village festivals both north and south of Rome—and likely enough at Rome too, though the city preferred to forget its primitive amusements as it grew into a metropolis. Unfortunately the tradition regarding the early Latin drama was vitiated by some early quasi-scholar—apparently Accius—who mingled futile hearsay with a line or two of an early record about Etruscan dancers and with the Aristotelian theory of how Greek drama grew up.[2] He mis-called this putative drama by the name *satura*. His story unfortunately became orthodox and displaced what might otherwise have survived of a truer tradition. The story is attributed to the year 364 B.C., a time at which no historical records were kept except for the dates and occasions of official priestly sacrifices. That is to say, the story is not worth repeating because it is attributed to a date when no records were kept of such events. All we know is that towns not far from Rome—and therefore presumably Rome as well—had simple drama before Livius began to translate Greek plays.

Such were the germs of the lyric, epic, and drama, vital and capable of growth when and if the

[2] See Hendrickson, "A Pre-Varronian Chapter of Roman Literary History," *Am. Jour. Phil.*, 1898, 285. Of the famous chapter in Livy (VII, 2) I should attribute only a scanty line regarding the Etruscan *ludii* to the *Annales Maximi*. The rest is unreliable reconstruction, since it refers to a period that antedates historical records by over a century. Many attempts have been made to enucleate the kernel of a dramatic history from the passage, but no one who has dealt with the historical sources of the fourth century can accept such attempts.

times should be favorable. But what is a favorable time? Why, for instance, had not literature come to life among others of the countless tribes about the Mediterranean except the Greeks and Hebrews? I ask, not to answer, but to emphasize the riddle. At Rome a few individuals were emerging from the group, the group was itself breaking out of its boundaries, but experiences were still modest. The citizens were chiefly quiet hard-working farmers who owned and tilled their plots; there was no seafaring commerce that brought tales of adventure from foreign lands, no colonizing beyond the seas, no traveling to foreign parts to bring the Latins a sense of awareness of their own place in the world. Society, as in any democracy where customs of the ruling clique are accepted by the rest, was passing through no strenuous changes, and no religious teacher from beyond the border was entering to shake tradition.

Then, in the third century B.C., came a very remarkable experience: the first great war with Carthage, fought for twenty-three years in Sicily, the victories of which compelled the whole civilized world of the day to recognize the existence of this hitherto unknown people and to invent plausible pedigrees for it. The construction of the first fleet and the sudden defeat of the greatest navy on the seas must have aroused the Romans to self-consciousness, as the Crusades aroused the French and the defeat of the Spanish Armada awakened Elizabethan England. This discovery of the Romans that they existed—that they were being watched and discussed—stirred them into a critical attitude about themselves. They saw that importance in the eyes of others implied expectations. And they discovered that, by the definition of the Greeks, they were barbarians and that the designation was deserved. They set about to learn avidly and to enter into the cultural occupations of the more advanced Greeks.

The first Messala, who had liberated Messana in the second year of the war, imported a painter to depict his victories on the walls of the senate house at Rome. Duilius who had defeated the Punic Armada was voted an honorary column with a long inscription modeled on the most verbose Sicilian laudations. But these are only some of the superficial effects of the new contacts. The Roman youth serving in Sicily was learning much more. Since the war lasted twenty-three years and since it required the services of practically all the able-bodied young men of Rome, these youths, who en-camped some six years each in and about the Greek towns of Sicily, carried home an abundance of im-pressions that meant much for the future of Rome. There can be little doubt that the tragedies of Euripides and the comedies of Menander were still being played at Syracuse and even in the smaller towns. Indeed Sicily had dramatic writers for many years after Athens had ceased to produce them. Mimes had long been a specialty of Sicily, and Theocritus was still writing them. Rhinton, for a while residing at Syracuse, was producing his farcical parodies of tragedies. Songs, too, tragical, comical, and sentimental were being sung with gestures, with dance and musical accompaniment on the variety stage of Sicilian towns. It was doubtless to satisfy the desires of soldiers who had seen these things that Roman officials immediately after the war introduced the production of Greek tragedies and comedies as a regular feature of the Roman festival. That all important date for Roman and world literature is 240 B.C.

With the war and pride in victory came also the need to write the nation's history in enduring form. In Sicily the Romans had discovered that they had become the object of wide observation. The Greeks, not knowing how to explain the amazing power of this small group of barbarians, had invented the legend that they must be a remnant of the Trojans. That legend had already found a place in the history of the Sicilian Timaeus, and the Sicilian city of Segesta, which claimed a similar pedigree, had made haste to assert cousinship with Rome, thus winning a favorable alliance with the victors. A pedigree at once so flattering to the Romans and so useful could hardly be disregarded. In less than a generation it came to be the accepted story at Rome— and Naevius, comprehending its literary purport, set out to write the epic of Rome with this legend as his preface. Rome had become conscious and expressive, the third of the western peoples to begin literary creation.

But progress in art is slow. In Greece there was a long silence after Homer. In England there were vast wastes with a few narrow garden spots in the five centuries between *Beowulf* and Chaucer. Rome had a scanty population of hard-working citizens constantly being recruited for war. After the First

Punic War there were frequent conflicts with Ligurians, Celts, and Illyrians. Then in 218 B.C. came the dreaded invasion of Hannibal. Every able-bodied man took up arms. The devastation of crops, the neglect of fields, the burden of taxes, the distressing gloom brought by a succession of defeats precluded all progress in literature. Only the theater continued to give one or two performances a year to grace the religious festivals.

In the middle of this war, in order to keep the Macedonian king from aiding Hannibal, Rome had entered a Greek coalition of states which were at enmity with Philip of Macedonia, and had thus come into close contact with Athens. When, therefore, the Greek states later appealed for aid to save democracy, a strong "philhellenism," aroused by such contacts and no less by the influence of Euripides and Menander on the Roman stage, brought about Rome's entrance into the Second Macedonian War.[3] Several men at Rome began (doubtless with the aid of secretaries) to write Roman histories in the Greek language. This does not mean that many Romans could read Greek with ease. It expressed, in a way, a desire that the cultured world should have some knowledge of what this "barbaric" state was accomplishing, and it was a gesture of deference to the one literature then known in the civilized world. Ennius also began to introduce such Greek prose works as he thought the people were ready for, the saws of "Epicharmus" and the cynical

[3] Historians who read only Polybius and Livy persist in denying that philhellenism was a factor in Roman politics. If they will but study the fragments of early Roman poetry they will emend their histories.

theology of Euhemerus. The directest result of philhellenism on literature was the demand for a closer approach to Greek models in the drama. Ennius' tragedies seem to have restored the Greek chorus, while in comedy men like Luscius and Terence presently vied with each other in claiming to be faithful translators of the Greeks.

In the early decades of the second century it appeared to some observers that Greek literature was about to overwhelm Rome. The younger nobility, led by Scipio Africanus, Flamininus, and their friends, was willing to employ all of Rome's man power and resources for the liberation of the Greeks from Macedonian rule, and when the Seleucid kingdom began to take advantage of the defeat of Philip and to subjugate the Greek cities of the Anatolian coast, these Romans challenged the great king with the ultimatum: "No Greek shall ever again anywhere be subject to foreign rule." Never has sentimentalism gone farther in foreign politics. It would not be an overstatement to find in the plays of Euripides produced in translation on the Roman stage the chief factor in this unreasonable wave of enthusiasm for a foreign cause.

But this love of things Greek—which resembles the English enthusiasm for French culture in the Restoration—overshot its mark. The armies that served in Greece and in Asia Minor learned foreign ways too rapidly and brought back too much. Livy (39.6), in a passage which accomplishes its purpose by a sarcastic juxtaposition of incongruous items, tells of the loaded trucks that the returning armies brought home.

There were couches with bronze frames, precious spreads, tapestries and other textiles, and whatever rare furniture could be found; tables with single supports and marble sideboards. Then it was that the Romans began to employ girls who danced and played bagpipes, and posturing houris to entertain guests at dinner. And the dinners were given with delicate care and expense. Cooks, who had formerly been the cheapest of servants, now gave way to expensive chefs, and a slave's task came to be considered an art.

We have no remains of houses of this period at Rome, but at Pompeii, which went through the same transformation because that seaport town profited by the commerce which Roman armies opened up in the east, we still may see the effects on architectural decoration initiated by this new reverence for things Greek. The lofty atrium of the houses of "Pansa" and "Sallust," roofed on splendid columns, the Basilica, the theater, and several temples about the Pompeian forum show what that contact with Greece meant to Italian architecture in the second century. Fresco painting had not yet come in, and it is likely that few houses used for wall decoration the oriental hangings mentioned by Livy. But the exquisite Alexander mosaic found in the "House of Pansa" reveals what domestic decoration could be, and the best furniture that has been found at Pompeii is made on patterns introduced from the Hellenized east at that time. In general, though not in all details, we can draw upon the second-century houses of Pompeii for a picture of a few at least of the new Hellenistic palaces that must have been erected at Rome after the Macedonian wars.

To complete the sketch we must also recall that this philhellenism was at first favorable toward eastern cults. The mystic cult of Bacchus, for instance, which apparently had its origin among the slaves brought to Rome from Tarentum and Locri during the last days of the Second Punic War,[4] was for several years allowed to spread undisturbed because so many of Rome's citizens had become accustomed to such things in Greece and Asia. With all these changes came also a laxity in manners and customs. Young men began to keep companions openly in the Greek manner. The Greek tutors engaged to teach young men Greek literature, rhetoric, and philosophy did not always inculcate respect for old Roman customs. In the Roman family, where woman enjoyed a freedom not known in Greece, new ideas of morality began to affect women as well as men, and since marriage was a contract and not a religious sacrament, bonds were easily loosened and divorces came to be of frequent occurrence. The reflection of these experiences we may observe faintly in the later plays of Plautus and abundantly in the earlier togatae.

All this resulted of course in a severe reaction not unlike the puritanic wave that swept over England after the catalysis of Elizabethan prosperity. Cato supported by many of the conservative nobles undertook to lead the revolt against philhellenism on every possible score. He attacked the foreign policy of the Scipios, which in his opinion wasted Rome's youth and resources without compensation for a sentimental cause, and the Scipionic group was

[4] See *Class. Quarterly*, 1927, 128.

accordingly stripped of political power. He attacked the returning generals for permitting the soldiers to be debauched by Greek vices; he directed an attack against the Bacchanalian cult till the senate passed a bill inflicting the death penalty upon those who persisted in furthering the cult; he used all the power of his censorship to degrade senators who had yielded to new customs and to conduct a rigid examination of the plate, furniture, and table expenses of his opponents.

Of course this drastic reform movement could not stop the cultural changes that were bound to come. Skepticism and sophistication can hardly be banished by legislation and law courts; but the outward signs of the new culture were for a season obscured. There is no doubt that Greek literature became less popular in the latter days of Cato. Such books as the "Sacred History" of Euhemerus were not again translated for a long time. Those who wished to read Greek poetry and philosophy had to confine themselves for many years to the originals; to put those things into Latin, to translate, paraphrase, or to write similar things in Latin, was not encouraged. Greek rhetoric might still be taught for the comprehension of Greek authors, but to put the Greek rules of rhetoric into Latin for general use was frowned upon. Greek tragedy in Roman adaptations—by Ennius and Pacuvius—had been established at the festivals so long that they remained, and, as adapted to the moral tone of the Romans by those dramatists, there could be little objection to them. But the efforts begun by Scipio Africanus to encourage such plays by making them

as inviting as possible to senators bore little fruit.
The permanent theater, for which a contract had
been let by the censors ten years after Cato's cru-
sade, was not completed, and when another effort
was made to complete it twenty years later the
senate had it torn down. Translated Greek comedies were still permitted at the festivals, but it
was necessary to indicate that the scene was Greek
and not Roman. Latin comedies, togatae—from our
point of view not a whit better in morals—then
came into fashion. To draw the crowd the authors
were permitted a certain freedom of expression but
here at least the vices were Roman and hence
pardonable.

Such were the effects of the puritanic, anti-
Greek reaction supported by Cato. It doubtless did
some harm to the drama by precluding the official
recognition that might have encouraged better work-
manship; it cast a shadow of disapproval over the
more delicate forms of literature which were associated in thought with Greece; it must bear some
of the blame for the fact that the century after
Cato is a period of prosaic nationalistic literature
in which no man of real genius appears. Direct
contact with the decadent Greeks of the day soon
destroyed the sentimental respect that the great
literature of classical Greece had created.

Meanwhile, however, a social change was in
progress which eventually affected literary production and the literary market at many points, and
particularly the drama and prose. I refer especially
to the silent movement which before the end of
the second century had largely eliminated the free

middle classes, substituting for them a slave economy of unusual proportions. When the Second Punic War began, though there were not a few rich nobles who lived in the city enjoying the fruits of country estates, the majority of the citizens were land-owning, working farmers of the type that we have known so well in our central and western states. At that time there was much free farm labor. Slave labor was also used to some extent, but since these slaves were usually of Italic race and thinly distributed they were well treated, indeed they were regarded as members of the family, as was customary with farm hands among the pioneers of our west. Such slaves usually were put in the way of some property with which they could buy their freedom; and with freedom came full citizenship.

The Second Punic War was the beginning of the end of this simple economy. Many small farmers went to the wall, farm labor became scarce because of the heavy casualties in the war. Hence investors often combined many small farms into large estates. At the end of the war, also, commissions were appointed by the State to draw in vast tracts that had been recovered from the Punic occupation in the south, and as colonists did not suffice for the settlement of these tracts much remained public land to be rented out in large estates for grazing. At the end of the war and during the next fifty years, hordes of war captives were brought to the block at Rome: Carthaginians, Iberians of Spain, Sardinians, Celts of the Po Valley, Macedonians, Illyrians, and Asiatics, and also many slaves that Greek owners were glad to sell on an expanding western market. These were bought cheaply, placed on the large estates and on ranches. With cheap labor it was possible to go into olive and vine culture and extensive cattle-raising. And with this capitalistic exploiting the small farmers found it difficult to compete. Many gave up the contest and moved to Cisalpine Gaul or overseas. The middle class of free folk began to dwindle. The few who knew how to adapt themselves to the new conditions acquired estates and lived in luxury. Naturally the hordes of slaves increased rapidly. In the cities also the slaves were increasing and driving out free labor, and they were slaves of foreign stock. Trained up to hard labor and an easy unconcern for morals, these slaves when they gained their freedom got the petty industries and shops in their control, and the citizen poor found it difficult to survive. This was a thoroughgoing social change that progressed silently and steadily through the second century and caused the Gracchi to launch a revolution in their vain attempt to bring back the conditions of a century before.

These changes—which in some respects remind us of conditions in our southern states before 1860—necessarily affected artistic production. At dramatic performances on Roman holidays the audience was of course gradually changing in type and quality and by no means for the better. The audiences to which public speeches were addressed—the speeches that had so much to do with shaping Latin prose style—were not the same in Caesar's day as in Cato's. And in view of the dwindling of the middle class, the class which usually provides the larger number of authors, we cannot be surprised if the dilettante production of the aristocratic writers and the hack work of servile producers fill a considerable space in the history of the late Republic. It is generally recognized, I think, that in our southern states between 1800 and 1860 literature fared badly, despite the orthodox argument that the existence of slave drudges gave leisure to genius to develop the nobler arts. Parasitic leisure has seldom employed its talents in artistic production.

This is one side of the social picture of the second century B.C.—the cheapening of the theatrical audiences at Rome which compelled a cheapening of the spectacles produced for them. At the same time, however, there was a rapid expanding beyond Rome of a reading public that spread with the gradual advance of the Latin language throughout Italy. For while in Cato's lifetime Latin was read only in Latium and in a few colonies, in Sulla's day the language was understood and used in almost every part of Italy from the Alps to the Greek cities of the southern coast. Hence while dramatic production was deteriorating in the theater at Rome, the non-dramatic literature of published books was winning an ever larger circle of readers. Furthermore, there was at the same time a deepening of cultural interests in the ruling class; for the nobles were becoming aware of their responsibilities as participants in world affairs, were finding a sounder education for their sons, were acquiring libraries and beginning to encourage literary effort. And since the nobles were constantly engaged in public service, their influence told especially in the field of history and forensic prose. This was in fact the period in which Rome's prose expression developed into a magnificent art.

This is a very brief sketch of the social changes that especially concern the student of republican literature, the details of which we shall try to notice more adequately when we reach the precise problems of each period. To the direct literary influence of specific Greek authors we need only refer at present, for that is less intangible and has frequently been discussed. That influence must not be minimized, for the Romans were generally as devoted to their predecessors as the Italians of the Renaissance were to the Romans, and the English Elizabethans were to the Italians, and they were as frank in acknowledging their debt. If this were a full history of Republican literature, we should have to give very many of its pages to an estimate of the Greek influences.

On the large question of what is called the racial character that is supposed to emerge in Rome's literature, I am convinced that it is too early to speak. Roman political, social, and religious behavior seem at times to justify the assumption of a certain homogeneity of mental and emotional traits in the Romans. Archaeology does not refute this assumption, for it sustains the view that the ancestral tribes invaded Italy in compact groups that may well have preserved inherited characters for a long period. Again the very fact that the Latin language had fairly well retained its very fragile declensional endings—which Latin lost quickly in the folk-mixture of the middle ages—would lend support to the theory that those tribes had long lived in groups relatively compact. Finally, anthropology seems ready to assume that in the later stone ages, before Europe was thickly settled by agrarians and before the arts of agriculture induced folk-movements in search of land, there was a slow emergence of several diverse peoples in different regions of Europe who, by processes of elimination and adaptation, had attained to what may fairly be called distinct racial peculiarities.[5] It is, therefore, scientific enough to assume the possibility of Latin or Italic traits of character, as distinguished, for instance, from Hellenic, Iberic, or Celtic.

During the Republic there is a certain similarity between the Catos, Fabii, Claudii, Metelli, Scipios, and the rest. From such men we expect prudence rather than speed of thought, a respect for courage rather than dash, for puritanic conduct rather than for unconventionality. We know them as generals who stuck at a campaign "if it took all summer," or many summers, as soldiers who refused to acknowledge defeat, as administrators who were sympathetic and patient with provincials but merciless to the disobedient, as lawmakers gifted with the knack of seeing the vital point at issue and reaching it in blunt phrases. They could be counted upon for sanity, stability, patience, and thoroughness.

[5] History has nothing to do with racial types classified by cranial measurements, for such typology deals with races that were mixed scores of thousands of years ago. The so-called Mediterranean, Alpine, and Nordic groups have for ages inherited the mixed nervous systems of each and all. The typology that concerns the historians of the ancient Mediterranean world is rather one of temperament and the various types grew out of segregated groups that shaped themselves during the few thousands of years that preceded the great European migrations of the second millenium B.C.

They expressed themselves better in architecture than in sculpture or painting; their lyricists and musicians were not numerous. They enjoyed comedy but it must be quick and pointed rather than subtle. They were peculiarly fond of tragedy but the theme must have dignity and purpose. Above all they loved good sound prose, in the histories of their nation told in periods worthy of the subject or in the long roll of the organ-voiced orator in the senate house.

It would, however, be misleading to stress these facts, which are more patent in public, social, and religious activity than in art. During the republic at least the literature is experimental, and it reveals many diverse tendencies, some of which did not survive in the Augustan day. While tragedy sought to continue the traditions of the best classical Greek work, it chose as its model the Euripidean tragedy with its more modern humanism rather than the older drama whose problems seemed to them archaic. Responding also to the social ideals of a more normal domestic life than old Greece possessed, Roman tragedy was somewhat more romantic in theme, and it broke up the Greek form in order to admit a larger space for the newer music. Comedy on the other hand neglected the Aristophanic type completely, building upon the social plays of Menander and his contemporaries. Rome took patriotism too seriously to care to have policies of state and august consuls ridiculed upon the stage. Yet the delicate art of Menander was not the goal of writers like Naevius and Plautus. His scrupulous respect for words, his fastidious striving toward a quiet contemplative expression of emotion, his insistence upon form, that directed its art toward the reader long after the first performance was forgotten, had made him more genuinely classic in effect than Aristophanes. The Roman dramatist wrote for a single performance, where effects must be translucent and immediate to an audience that was used to the robust fun of homemade plays. Plautus has no connections with rigorously classical ideals. He cares for spontaneous, natural, paganly human laughter.

The Roman lyric of the Republic also rejects classification. Before the Greek lyric reached Rome the great singers of Greece had already been forgotten by decadent Athens as thoroughly as seventeenth-century England had forgotten Chaucer. When the Romans began to study lyrical forms they apparently did not even hear the names of Sappho and Alcaeus; they were told about the dainty epigrams of Alexandria, and they began to copy these. Aedituus and Laevius might as well have lived at Samos. Catullus at first fed on the same fare, but one stirring experience set him free. Thereafter he wrote songs that no Greek could have claimed. They have the lilt, beauty, and precision of his models, but a natural freedom, a lucidity, and a convincing passion that make the epigrams of the Garland seem lucubratory. They obviously spring out of a society that is less artificial and out of a life that grows in a young world.

Lucretius again refuses to fall into a conventional pattern. He has no standards, no proportions, no models. The early Greeks had staidly versified science so that it might easily be memorized. That was not Lucretius' purpose. Alexandrians had versified science again because the interest in the subject had become general. Lucretius wrote for a public that had cared little for science, but he wrote with the zeal of a prophet because he could not keep silent, and his voice was heard. His work has no unity, no controlling plan or single mood. He hurls his bald facts, his images, his logic, and his pleas indiscriminately. There is nothing else in Greece or Rome like him. And so we might go on.

What are the Romans of the republic? When we read their political history we feel a unity of spirit and are prone to say that we understand them. This may be because of a certain racial trait or perhaps because a certain limited aristocracy set the traditions early which became so binding that political activity followed the *mos majorum*. But the men who entered literature were not of one class nor did they express the ideals of any one group. They came out of different strata of different localities and spoke for different mores. Whatever we may say we must admit that the really personal literature of the republic was neither conformist nor monotonous, neither Greek nor classical in spirit. It was frankly experimental, but it always proves to reflect some phase of Roman life.

CHAPTER II

EARLY TRAGEDY AND EPIC

Browning has recalled the story of how Greek war captives taken at Syracuse in the Peloponnesian war earned their release by reciting snatches from the plays of Euripides. It was a century and a half after that seige that the Romans came to Sicily in the First Punic War, and the city was still interested in the old drama, indeed was now taking its part in producing tragedies. One of the last of the dramatists, one of the so-called "Pleiad," was a Syracusan of Hiero's time, and King Hiero was himself so devoted to the drama that he even built a theater for Agyrion, a petty village on the border of his small kingdom. We have noticed how the Roman youth who campaigned year after year in Sicily learned something of the arts of civilization and on their return home created a demand for the things they had come to enjoy while abroad. The year after the victorious troops returned from Sicily, Livius, a schoolmaster of Greek origin, staged a translation of a Greek tragedy as a supplement to the annual chariot race. This production marks the beginning of Rome's education in letters. There must be some close connection between this homecoming of the army, and the performance of Livius' play, for the change in character of a great religious festival could not have been suggested by a freedman. The magistrates responsible for the performance were senators and the senate had of course requested the play. In all likelihood it was also the senate that invited King Hiero of Syracuse to Rome to see the games; for he, if any one, would have been asked to supply some actor to help stage the first play, and it was only appropriate that he should come to inaugurate the new era of culture.

From that time on plays were produced every year. Five years after the first performance, Naevius, who had served in the Sicilian campaigns (and had perhaps learned Greek there), began to help in the work of adapting Greek plays for the Roman stage. Only brief fragments of those early plays have survived and in reviewing the list of titles we might wonder at the enthusiasm they reveal for plays shaped on the old Greek mythology. But the predominance of titles derived from the Trojan cycle explains this enthusiasm. It was in Sicily that the Roman soldiers had learned the Greek story of how Rome had been founded by Trojan refugees. The stories of Hector, of the Trojan horse, Achilles, Ajax, Iphigenia, and the rest were therefore not without personal interest in the barbaric city. The unlettered shoemakers, smiths, and carpenters at Rome, men whose modern equals could hardly be expected to sit patiently through a performance of Gilbert Murray's *Trojan Women*, eagerly listened to the half-comprehended lines of Livius' translation. They had been told that these were the stories of their long-lost ancestors.

Livius is merely a name, which is unfortunate, since we know that he deserved well of Roman civilization. Naevius is less shadowy, a personality whose creative work left an impress on such powerful men as Cicero and Vergil two centuries later. He wrote not only plays, but an epic, condensing Rome's history in an annalistic poem, the climax of which was the great victory over Carthage in which he had had a share. From the sixty scattered lines of this epic rescued by late lexicographers we do not quite find the justification for Vergil's high regard. There is no poetry in them. But grammarians pick their lines to illustrate linguistic usage and not for effective phrasing. Even Shakespeare becomes prose if judged by the citations found in Webster. However, for the preservation of the metrical schemes employed by Naevius we are grateful. Though he had used a large variety of Greek meters for his drama, he did not in his epic. Here he preserves the native Saturnian line that had been used in religious songs, and apparently in ballads. That he did not adopt a standard Greek meter for his epic, as he did for his tragedies and comedies, is proof enough that the old native narrative verse was fully established in a well-known body of poetry which we have lost.

In many respects this verse resembles the old English line that relies upon alliteration and rhythmic ictuses which balance each other in the two severed parts of the line:

In a sómer séson whan sóft was the sónne.

But the Saturnian had six ictuses instead of four, and as Latin verse was more aware of its quantities

and less of its word stress than English the ictuses,
while somewhat regardful of word accent, were more
attentive to quantity. Finally, since alliteration is
more effective when the ictus falls on the first
syllable, and since the Latin accent had to a large
extent shifted away from the first syllable by the
time of Naevius, the use of alliteration was somewhat
less frequent in Naevius than in *Beowulf*. In Vergil's day the effect of this verse must have been
somewhat like that of Langland's poems upon the
Elizabethans. The shift of the Latin word accent
toward the penult was already destroying the effectiveness of the verse even when Naevius wrote;
and the break of the line in the center rendered it
ineffective for sustained narration. Its halting movement may be somewhat inadequately illustrated by
a paraphrase of Naevius' own epitaph:

If death of any mortal   sadden hearts immortal,
The heavenly Muses surely   Naevius' death bemoan;
For after he departed   to the shades of Orcus
The voice of Rome is silent   music is forgotten.

Ennius abandoned the line, and it was eventually
doomed, just as the Anglo-Saxon meters in England
began to disappear when the richer rhythms of
French poetry came to be appreciated.

It was Naevius also who broke away from Greek
subjects in the drama, though with what success we
cannot say. He made what we may call a "chronicle
play" of the Romulus legend which disregarded the
conventional unities, and he also wrote a pageantry
play to commemorate the heroic single combat of
Marcellus with a Celtic chieftain. He is therefore
among the first to stage contemporary drama and

to disregard the restrictions of time and place. That he made the same innovations in comedies like his *Hariolus* is probable but cannot be proved from the few lines that remain.

An independent creator he was and might have carried progress far had not so large a part of his activity fallen in the restraining period of the Second Punic War. His end was in character. Accustomed to speak his mind freely in his comedies, he vigorously supported the Fabian policy when it was unpopular, and after the group supporting Scipio, which demanded a more aggressive conduct of the war, came into power, he continued his sarcastic criticism of the Scipionic group. Rome had always tolerated free speech, but even at Rome patience was short in war time. War censorship discovered an old law which, with a little imaginative interpretation, could be stretched to cover the case of this satirist.[1] Only one line has survived of the satiric comedy which referred to the fact that Metellus, a friend of Scipio's, had taken advantage of a fortuitous circumstance to stand for the consulship. He was elected through no desert of his own. The point of the line—Fato Metelli Romae fiunt consules—rests on a *double entendre*, because *fato* may be construed either as ablative or as dative, while *Romae* may be genitive or locative. The line therefore may mean either:

"The Metelli became consuls at Rome by chance,"

which is hardly a flattering remark, or what is even less flattering:

"The Metelli became consuls to Rome's sorrow."

[1] *Am. Jour. Phil.*, 1927, 105.

The Metelli apparently thought Naevius meant to suggest both, which is likely enough, and they succeeded in having him imprisoned, and eventually banished. He seems to have found a home in Carthage, the land of the enemy against whom he had once fought.

These two dramatists, for reasons which must be discussed later, increased the use of musical accompaniment in tragedy and comedy. In Euripides the body of the drama had been in recited trimeters. The choral parts were of course sung to the accompaniment of rhythmical movements called dance, and there was also music when the actors engaged in dialogue with the chorus, as well as in some of their monologues. But the musical element had been reduced very much during the century that followed Euripides when the drama had gradually dispensed with the chorus even in the staging of Euripides. Rome was then too primitive to provide the twelve or more trained singers and dancers that even the later Greeks had found beyond their resources. Livius indeed had experienced such difficulty in securing actors with good voices that he himself took the leading rôle, and, not adequately gifted for the singing parts, he tried, we are told, the inartistic device (not unknown on our comic stage) of placing a singer beside the musician to carry the melody of the lyric parts while he acted and presumably recited the lines of the songs. That was, of course, only a temporary makeshift, but it shows how difficult it was to provide satisfactory artists at the time. It would seem then that since these early writers found it impossible to produce choruses adequately because these required the elaborate training of many singers in intricate musical compositions, they compensated as best they could by increasing the number of monodies in their plays, writing them in a few well-defined meters, such as the septenarii, cretics, and bacchiacs,[2] which were not too difficult to learn. Thus it was that Roman tragedy became even more like modern opera than the tragedy of the Greek stage had been. These early men of Rome, who mean so little to us, had developed a form which was capable of carrying on the work of Greek tragedy on a primitive stage, and capable also of growing into a richer drama as soon as the resources of the small city should permit. They made the drama possible for Rome.

As a composer of tragedies and epic verse, Ennius succeeded Naevius, but, writing in an era of enthusiastic philhellenism, he came near yielding too much to a great foreign influence. Had he not been a man of remarkable poetic powers his example might well have quenched the spirit of Rome in the rising literature. One of the first Latin authors that we would ask the excavators of Herculaneum to restore to us is Ennius. No single work of his has survived. Of his twenty-five or more tragedies we possess only about four hundred lines; of the eighteen books of *Annals* a little over five hundred complete lines;

[2] Livius and Naevius were both very fond of the septenarii; the iambic tetrameter appears in the tragic fragments of Naevius once; cretics are found in the *Equos Trojanus*, and bacchiacs apparently in Naevius' *Danae* and in his *Lycurgus*. Fraenkel, *Hermes* (1927), 357 ff., has shown that the trochaic septenarius (quadratus) was an old Latin meter. We need not, however, assume with him that it was derived from the Greek. As a marching rhythm it is too natural to require explanation. The assumption of an Indo-European *Urvers* needs to be exiled from our books. Song and dance are very old.

of his satires, his *Euhemerus* and his *Epicharmus*, not enough fragments have survived to give us a very clear idea of the scope of each. All in all we have about three per cent of his work in scraps, but here at least there are several connected passages cited in appreciation of something else than the grammatical usages they illustrate.

Ennius too, like Naevius, told Rome's story in verse. One's impulse is to discount the accuracy of any history that employs artifice. And one must grant of course that a poet will select his incidents with a view to their dramatic values and picturesqueness. One must remember, however, that poetry had a serious place in all early literature for the reason that, before the day of much writing, all teachable things, even history and philosophy, were put into verse for mnemonic purposes. The works of Solon and Heracleitus would not have contained different matter if they had been put into prose. In Ennius' day many national histories that purported to be accurate were composed in verse. And Ennius probably did not permit himself to include fictive incidents in his *Annals*, nor has he been proved incorrect at any point.[3] Cicero cited him for the gist of the famous speech of Appius Claudius, and added as a matter of indifference that the original of the speech was in existence. Apparently Ennius' summary was accurate enough so that it was not necessary to refer to the original text.

The influence of his *Annals* was in its field comparable to that of Homer. From Ennius all schoolboys got their first impressions of what Rome's

[3] See *Cambridge Ancient History*, VII, 644.

great heroes had accomplished. He was unsurpassed as a painter of character. With a few telling strokes he revealed the essential traits of those strong, bold, tireless heroes who made the old Republic irresistible in power, magnificent in tradition, and a saving inspiration in the days of decadence. He was near to these men, and it was as he saw them that they lived on in memory and still live on. He made Roman character memorable in the two lines on Fabius Maximus:

> Unus homo nobis cunctando restituit rem:
> Noenum rumores ponebat ante salutem.

and in the single line on Curius:

> Quem nemo ferro potuit superare nec auro.

His epic was an exposition of the text he himself devised so effectively:

> Moribus antiquis res stat Romana virisque:

And it was Ennius who more than any one else kept Roman society upon that foundation.

We happen to be able to test his influence by what he did with the portrait of Pyrrhus. Only a generation before Ennius was born this picturesque enemy of Rome had had a friendly alliance with the Messapian tribe to which Ennius himself belonged. The poet, therefore, had heard much about the king. Pyrrhus, in fact, had some very sympathetic traits of character, a remarkable chivalry, and a certain sense of honor and loyalty such as is often found in the chieftains of primitive folk. These qualities stand out in the characterization of him that Ennius has left us; and these are the outstand-

ing traits that we find in all the later Roman references to Pyrrhus. That Ennius should have responded to these qualities is not strange, but that
all the rest of the Romans should thus enthusiastically have lauded an enemy who nearly wrecked
Rome is less to be expected. The explanation is of
course that what Ennius wrote colored the historic
conceptions of all who followed. This becomes evident when we read Plutarch, a Greek, and his
biography of Pyrrhus. When drawing upon Roman
sources for the Italian campaign of the king, Plutarch paints the same picture as Ennius, but when
he draws upon Greek authors in describing the
Greek campaigns, he reveals the fact that the
knightly hero of the Roman historians had a less
charming side which certain close observers at home
were well aware of. Like all historians Ennius had
his enthusiasms, and he had such power of portraiture that not a trait blurred.

He was also fair. Pyrrhus got his meed of
praise, but the opponents of Pyrrhus, Fabricius
and Appius Claudius, were characterized with equal
sympathy. Of his own contemporaries, Fabius the
Slow-goer was effectively portrayed as we have seen,
and Cato "in caelum tollitur," as Cicero affirms,
although Scipio Africanus, who was bitterly opposed
by these conservatives, became, as he deserved to
be, the outstanding hero of the book.

It was entirely appropriate that, for his heroic
narrative, Ennius borrowed the dactylic hexameter
of the Greeks, but it was after all a daring thing to
do, since meters seldom transplant with success.
However, Naevius' use of the native Saturnian had

demonstrated its inability to carry heroic narrative. Imagine *Paradise Lost* crammed into the primitive English rhythms of Langland! The dactylic hexameter was in Greek regularly associated with the epic. It had one disadvantage in its requirement of a larger proportion of short syllables than normal Latin writing contained, but that was overcome by simply permitting more spondees than Homeric custom had enjoyed. This resulted in a reduction of tempo which after all suited Roman military movement. There was another difficulty which was more serious. While Greek verse needed to give little attention to word accent, the Latin word accent was jealous of attention. With the relative fixity of the accent, it was impossible to write Latin dactyls based both upon quantity and word-accent. Ennius nevertheless ventured upon an experiment. That he had a very delicate ear for the demands of the Latin language is proved by the careful adjustments in his dramatic senarii, where adjustments were not easy to make. He would not have foisted impossible dactyls upon Rome. The fact that he wrote quantitative dactyls and continued to write them, and that his *Annals* lived for centuries is proof that he did not overstep the bounds of good taste. The explanation of his success is probably that the word stress in the Latin of his day was so moderate that a conflict with the ictus was not fatal to aesthetic pleasure if only it fell upon long syllables, and also that during the forty years of dramatic performances at Rome, the ears of the audiences had become trained under the influence of music to disregard such conflicts in the many lyric rhythms, including dactyls. By his sensible modification of the Homeric line, Ennius created as great a resource for Latin poetry as Chaucer did for English poetry, and shaped for Vergil's use "the stateliest measure ever moulded by the lips of man."

Ennius began to write tragedies about 200 B.C. at the very time when philhellenism was at its height. Being a man of wide culture who knew his Greek well he readily responded to the general demand for things Greek. Though he produced one play (*The Rape of the Sabine Women*) on a Roman theme, and a pageantry play called the *Ambracia* to commemorate the victory of a friend during the war with Aetolia, he seems to have striven chiefly to reproduce on the Roman stage the effects of Euripides' tragedies. And now that the restraints of poverty had become somewhat relaxed, and the drama had continued long enough to foster a certain amount of skilful talent for its interpretation, he was freer to present his tragedies more nearly in the old Greek manner. It has accordingly been plausibly conjectured[4] that it was Ennius who reintroduced the chorus so that the Greek plays might be given without cutting. There is no reason for supposing that the choral song in the *Thyestes* (written in bacchiacs) or the one in the *Medea* (octonarii) or the one in the *Iphigenia* (septenarii) were recited by a single singer. It is clear from the fragments that in several of his plays, notably in the *Achilles*, the *Eumenides*, the *Hector*, and the *Hecuba*, choral groups were actually participants in the plays as they had been in the Greek originals.

[4] See Duckett, *Studies in Ennius*, 56, who revises the views of Leo, *De Tragoedia Romana* (Göttingen, 1910).

And since in the plays of his successor, Accius, it can be demonstrated that a chorus sang, we ought to accept the reasonable interpretation of the Ennian fragments and attribute to this philhellenist the importation of choral song into Roman tragedy. Ennius, however, deferred to Roman taste so far as the rhythms were concerned. He adhered largely to the lyric meters which Livius and Naevius had popularized, and seldom attempted to employ the more intricate systems of the Greeks.[5] That Ennius was as successful in his tragedies as in his epic is adequately proved by the fact that many of his plays were still being produced a century after his death and were avidly read by men like Cicero.

Pacuvius, the nephew and successor of Ennius, did not write many plays. From the little that remains of his work we should judge that he preferred themes somewhat off the beaten track and that in choosing plays that contained heterodox discussions of ethical themes, he, too, felt the influence of the new Greek learning and kept in mind the interests of the intellectualist at Rome. The grammarians have also noticed the fact that his lyric meters paid more attention to Latin word stress than those of his predecessors.[6] They cite particularly his care in composing anapaests with caesuras in such a way that long initial syllables fell under the ictus. These anapaests in fact read like dactyls with an anacrusis of two shorts at the beginning. This innovation decidedly proves that the poet had

[5] For a strophic system in Ennius, see Crusius, *Philologus*, Supp. XXI, 114.

[6] *Gram. Lat. Keil*, VI, 77, 7; Vollmer, *Röm. Metrik*, in Gercke's *Einleitung*, I, 8, p. 6; however among the preserved fragments of Pacuvius there are several anapaests that resemble those of Ennius.

a precise ear and desired to attain harmonious effects. His successors showed that they appreciated his innovation, but they occasionally used the old turbid lines to express emotional excitement.

The most successful of the writers of tragedy was Accius, a poet who spanned the era between the Gracchans and the Social War. We have fragments of more than forty tragedies from his busy pen, and many of his plays were re-staged in Cicero's day. He was the favorite of the great actors, Aesopus and Roscius. He did not depart far from the customs laid down by Ennius in respect to meters, music, and chorus, but the fact that he freely readapted the Greek plays which furnished themes to his predecessors can only mean that he used the same liberty in giving his own interpretation to old plots that Euripides had used in treating anew the myths that had been staged by Aeschylus and Sophocles. We happen to know from the remarks of Terence that convention did not permit the staging of more than one paraphrase of any given Greek play. When, therefore, Accius writes plays upon familiar themes we must assume that he is offering something essentially original in his interpretation of the old plot. In fact we find good evidence of his original treatment in the fragments. So, for instance, in his *Antigone* he changed the personnel of the chorus (as Ennius had done in the *Iphigenia*), which implies that the purpose of the play was altered. It is also clear that Accius made free to disregard the conventional unities of place and time, for in the *Brutus* there are scenes laid in Gabii, in Ardea, and in Rome.

All these dramatists apparently altered their originals freely in order to make the story and its meaning more plausible to a Roman audience. The *Medea* of Ennius reveals many changes of this kind. For instance, the Latin author felt that he must prepare the audience early in the play for the gruesome death of the children,[7] a detail unnecessary in Euripides, who wrote for an audience that knew the plot. This kind of thing must have occurred frequently. Again, Ennius had to alter Medea's long monologue, since before a Roman audience accustomed to seeing a matron in public, there was no point in making her apologize for appearing outside of the palace.[8] Ennius has here been needlessly accused of misunderstanding the Greek original! Ennius knew his Greek; he had learned it at school in Tarentum. His alterations were introduced to suit the psychology of his own audience. Similar changes are numerous and need not be dwelt upon.

The alteration of the very purport of the plays is of more importance to us. For instance, Atreus, the old Greek tyrant of primitive brutality, was calculated to offend Roman taste. It is apparent from the fragments of Accius that it was the sufferings of Thyestes rather than the daring of Atreus which received sympathetic attention—a fact not surprising in a city where the word *rex* was feared and hated. Euripides' story of Andromeda had a matter-of-fact plot in which Andromeda's father begged Perseus to slay the dragon and to rescue his daughter. This plot followed the myth and was expected in Athens. But not so at Rome. In Accius'

[7] Ennius, ed. Vahlen, *Scaenica*, 272.
[8] See *Am. Jour. Phil.* 1913, 326.

play Perseus is rather the chivalrous knight; he
rescues the lady first and then pleads for her hand.
Similarly, in the *Clytemestra* of Accius one also finds
a very modern note, for Accius suggests that if
Agamemnon's inconstancy could be excused because
of his long separation from his wife, Clytemestra
might possibly have the benefit of the same argument. In the *Andromache* of Ennius and the *Asty-
anax* of Accius there is an intense note of sorrow
for the child of Hector and Andromache that
reminds one of Vergil's lines in the third book of
the Aeneid. This is a Roman strain deriving from
the Romans' claim to be descended from the Trojans.
In the *Phoenissae* of Accius the motivation of the
whole play is changed by representing Eteocles
breaking a command rather than a personal pledge.
In the *Eurysaces* of Accius we have a slightly different reason for the use of Roman motive. This play
was re-staged by the great actor Aesopus when
Cicero was in exile, because of its picture of the
unjust banishment of Telamon. The Roman audience appreciated the possible allusion to Cicero's
suffering and cheered Aesopus' lines to the echo.
Accius may well have written it originally and introduced the changes in order to influence his audience
and obtain the recall of some political exile like
Popilius, about 130 B.C. The lines have a genuine
Roman ring.

In our own day when every dramatist is compelled to create a new plot it is easy to underesti-
mate the originality of men like the Greek Euripides,
the Roman Accius, the French Racine, the English
Shakespeare, who all in varying degrees were satis-

fied to use old plots, even old plays, and to give all their attention to a personal and original interpretation of the inner meaning of a familiar story and of the motives that impelled the characters. We may illustrate the old method of procedure by examining Seneca's *Medea*, since here we have a complete Latin play which shows what even an uninspired Roman dramatist might do by way of re-reading an ancient legend. Medea in the old unvarnished myth of the barbaric age was apparently a bundle of natural passions, a savage creature gifted with superhuman powers. Jason owed her his life, but since a Greek prince could hardly wed a barbarian and make her his queen, he might reasonably, according to Greek standards, abandon her when his "higher" duties to state and position demanded it. In a rage of jealous hate, the creature might then wreak her vengeance upon Jason and Jason's children. Such action was quite comprehensible to the semibarbarous age that shaped the myth, but not to the more humane Athenians of Euripides' day. The Greek dramatist, accordingly, had offered a new explanation of the problem. In his version Jason has disregarded the higher demands of humanity for a selfish passion or a more selfish ambition. Medea, the woman, has been infinitely wronged, and in her helplessness—it is not all jealousy and hate—she slays her children to save them from a worse fate. But to the Roman even this interpretation seems impossible, and the character of Jason least comprehensible of all. A Roman nobleman could not so abandon his sons, and the woman, if she was indeed human, could not slay her children either in hate or in love. Seneca, therefore, while keeping the main plot, seeks a new explanation for the woman's act. Medea is again painted as the barbaric witch that she was before Euripides transformed her. Jason marries Creusa for the sake of his children—a wholly comprehensible act to a Roman of Nero's day—and the uncontrollable Medea is driven into a rage that does not hesitate to commit murder. But, however jealous she might have been, Seneca feels that she could not have laid hands upon her own offspring. Yet the tale said that she did. Seneca's solution of the dilemma is simple. Woe has driven Medea insane and the ghost of her brother hovers before her, a symbol of that insanity. Accordingly, it is in a fit of madness that she does the deed. In Seneca, as in Euripides, the action follows the ancient myth, but the interpretation of that myth varies with the author, and in both cases this reinterpretation is not so much an invention of the dramatist as a reflection of the changed point of view of the society of his time. The moderns have, of course, felt the same need for a re-reading of the story as the widely differing versions of Grillparzer and Catulle Mendéz demonstrate. This is but one simple illustration of how the Roman dramatists could re-stage old myths and yet constantly invite the audience to something new. The emphasis upon the interpretation rather than upon the plot is precisely the same as it was in the days of Racine and Shakespeare.

How far the Roman dramatists were indebted to predecessors for their very striking employment of song is still a moot problem. Leo,[9] following a

[9] Leo, *Die plautinischen Cantica* (1897).

suggestion of Crusius, held that the Plautine cantica followed the manner of the contemporary music-hall lyrics of Greece as illustrated by the then recently discovered "Grenfell song." This theory was rejected by Fraenkel[10] because he found no vital similarity between the Grenfell fragment and the Plautine cantica. In his view the Roman predecessors of Plautus—Livius and Naevius—who paraphrased both tragedy and comedy, had probably developed the cantica in tragedy from Euripidean models and then employed them in comedy as well. This theory has a certain plausibility but cannot yet be tested because the cogent examples of cantica in tragedy must be drawn from Ennius, who was not a predecessor but rather a tardy contemporary of Plautus. The view of Leo has received some little support from a brief and peculiar mime-fragment of the British Museum recently published by Milne.[11] However this fragment is so late that it may represent post-Plautine developments, and therefore cannot be pressed into decisive service. It must also be added that recent studies tend to show that Greek New Comedy of the time of Menander had not wholly given up the use of strophic lyrics,[12] and that the Plautine and Ennian cantica themselves seem to have retained not a few traces of strophic structure.[13]

Without attempting to solve a problem for which too many of the quantities are still unknown, I would only wish to suggest the need of considering

[10] Fraenkel, *Plautinisches im Plautus* (1922), criticized by Immisch, *Sitz. Heid. Akad.* 1923.

[11] Milne, *Cat. of lit. pap. in British Mus.* 1927 (no. 52); cf. Wuest and Croenert, *Philol.* 1928, 153 ff.

[12] See Marx's ed. of *Rudens*, 254 ff.

[13] Crusius, *Die Responsion in den plaut. Cantica* (1929).

the practical factors of Roman experience and of Roman exigencies when we try to explain the Roman trend toward an operatic form. In the first place it is well to keep in mind that Naevius, who dominated the Roman theater for thirty years of its formative period, had campaigned in Sicily long enough to become the first annalist of the Punic war. Practically every city of Sicily where Roman troops were stationed had a theater, and in the days of Hiero the demand for dramatic entertainment in Sicily was so vigorous that new theaters were being built. We still have evidence[14] of Hellenistic theaters at Syracuse, Tauromenium, Segesta, Tyndaris, Akrae, Catania, and Agyrion. It is agreed that the Greek tragedies and comedies that were then being produced—the plays that Naevius probably saw—were generally devoid of choruses. The elaborate choruses of the tragedies had fallen away, partly because of the cost of staging them, and partly doubtless because new musical fashions had grown impatient of the somewhat academic formalism of the strophic songs.[15] In comedy, considerations of the expense and a desire for scope and freedom in choosing theme and form in song worked toward the same end. There can be little doubt that in Sicily Naevius saw performances of postclassical tragedies and comedies, not to mention music-hall performances of mimes and farces, that gave him good suggestions as to how the plays of Euripides could be staged without a chorus, and

[14] See Bieber, *Denkmäler d. Theaterwesen* and Bulle, *Abh. Bayer. Akad.* 1928.

[15] If Horace's strictures on the new music of the drama in the *Ars Poet.* 200–15 took a hint from Neoptolemus, we may suppose that Hellenistic critics had objected to this change.

how a paraphrase of a Menandrian comedy that had lost its *entr'acte* songs could be turned into something like light opera. And a genius as inventive and independent as Naevius would soon break through the limitations of the Roman stage and shape, with the help of such suggestions, a performance suited to Roman needs.

But even if the Sicilian performances offered suggestions of how to stage comedies and tragedies without choruses it seems to have been the Romans who made the old classics conform to the new method and in doing so greatly enlarged rather than diminished the scope of the musical accompaniment. The second reason for this increase in songs seems to me, therefore, to lie in the need for music to help carry the new meters which dramatic writing demanded. Latin had been as poor in meters as early English was later. The chief drudge of all work had been the Saturnian verse, a form unfit for either sustained narrative or for realistic dialogue. Its line was slow and reflective. It had been used for ritual song, for funeral elegy, for lullabies, for gnomic poetry, and apparently also for lampoons; but it was as unfit for the drama as Ennius had found it to be for epic narration. There was also apparently a lively marching verse, the quadratus, the meter with which we are familiar from the trochaic tetrameters of the Greeks and from the lines of Tennyson's *Locksley Hall*:

> With the standards of the peoples plunging through
> the thunder storm.

At least critics are now ready to accept the remark of Horace that lines like

Rex erit qui recte faciet, qui non faciet, non erit,

were sung in the days of old Camillus. Whenever
we happen to have a fragment of a soldier's song
quoted in Latin it is in this quick step:

Ecce Caesar nunc triumphat, qui subegit Gallias.

That meter had possibilities in the drama, and it
was very freely used, though it doubtless had to be
weaned away from its boisterous military associations. For rapid action and excitement it served
well. It appears that early tragedy felt that it
belonged to music and used it in lyric passages, in
recitative chants as well as in dramatic speeches.
Naevius was very fond of it.

Tragedy, however, needed an easy line of moderate length for its ordinary dialogues, and several
meters in different moods to carry the monologues,
songs, and emotional dialogues. For these Livius
and Naevius, as we have noticed, had taken over
and adapted a large number of Greek verse-forms.
Now the adaptation of a foreign meter is a very
serious matter. It took English poetry hundreds of
years to merge French and old English rhythms, as
it took France centuries to find a satisfactory adaptation of the medieval Latin systems. The labor of
reshaping Greek meters for use in Latin was all
the more difficult at the time because the Latin
language happened to be just then at a critical
point in its accentual development. The Greek
word-accent had but very slight stress, so that
quantity was permitted to determine verse-rhythm.
In Latin, also, the quantity of the vowel and the
syllable was still the dominant element at this time,

indeed determined the position of the word accent, and was responsible for the penultimate accent rule that prevailed in most words during the century in which Naevius wrote. Latin must have been nearly as precise in the observance of longs and shorts as Greek. But the difficulty was that the stress of the word accent had also been a marked factor in Latin pronunciation for some time. Now in forming or introducing new rhythms the Latin poets would have to choose either stress or quantity as the decisive element on which to build and force the other element to comply. This is a choice that very few languages have imposed upon their poets. In English there was of course no such decision necessary since our accent remained a strong stress while our syllabic quantities, in the mingling of Germanic and French, became so completely confused that the values of half of them are hardly determinable by ear. This difference between Latin and English has not always been given due weight. When, for instance, the late Poet Laureate of England assumed that the quantitative meters of Ennius and Vergil resemble in effect the quantitative meters that he composed in English, he disregarded the vital difference between the two languages.[16]

---

[16] Robert Bridges, *Ibant Obscuri*. Such hexameters as

> They were amid the shadows by night in loneliness obscure
> Walking forth i' the void and vasty dominyon of Ades:
> As by an uncertain moonray secretly illumin'd—

do not represent what happened to Latin in Ennius, for the reason that in Latin pronunciation the quantity was the dominant element controlling even the accent. In English the reverse is true. Fraenkel, *Iktus und Akzent*, has recently committed a similar mistake in judgment, influenced apparently by the high respect that speakers of German must necessarily have for stress. He has resorted to daring hypotheses in trying to prove that Plautus always correctly observes a species of stress (see Sonnenschein in *Class. Quart.*, 1929, 81). It is significant

While in Latin quantities were readily distinguished even by the rabble, a fact that is shown by the emergence of the penultimate law before there were any teachers, in English it requires a laboratory apparatus to decide what really is the length of certain syllables. On the other hand, stress is dominant in English and unmistakable in all colloquial speech, whereas in Latin it was so moderate in the new position it had recently acquired that for many centuries after Plautus it had very little effect upon the morphology of the language. Apparently the first Roman poets chose as wisely as could be expected in determining to base their meters upon quantity rather than upon word-stress. But in doing so they had to face a serious dilemma: a stress-accent does not like to be disregarded, and ultimately (six centuries later) it asserted itself and insisted upon dominance. The quadratus, or trochaic tetrameter, which apparently grew up before the Romans knew Greek or grammar, had made a compromise that satisfied the ear. It looked to quantity as the dominant element, placing the verse-beat invariably upon a long (or its equivalent), but it by no means wholly disregarded word accent. In the lines of soldiers' songs that survived, it is not often that word accent is slighted more than once in a line, and Ennius, Naevius, and Plautus in their plays seldom permitted themselves to neglect it more often than twice in a spoken line.

In "Rex erit qui recte faciet, qui non faciet,

that the French, who feel little stress in their diction, go to the other extreme and find stress insignificant in Latin. Latin in fact was like neither; it resembled Hungarian in being primarily quantitative, and in its word accent had a moderate stress not without a rather noticeable pitch such as is found in some parts of Sweden.

non erit," aside from the last syllable which of course is hidden in a falling cadence, only *erit* at the beginning, an unemphatic word, gets what may be called a mechanical accent. But this smoothness is natural chiefly in the trochaic meter and it occurs here because the normal penultimate accent of Latin, which stresses a long syllable next to the final, is by nature adapted to a trochaic quantitative rhythm. Obviously an iambic line can take advantage of all the qualities of the trochaic line if the poet will so adapt the first word as to secure a trochaic swing in the rest of the line. Livius was very skilful in adapting the Greek trimeter to the spirit of the Latin trochaic. He increased the caesuras—that is he freely cut the iambic foot in two—not for the sake of caesuras but in order that by cutting iambic feet he could create a trochaic rhythm which would operate easily with a penultimate accent; he permitted resolved longs in any position except the last foot, because when the penult is short the antepenult receives the accent, and a fair coincidence of accent and ictus is again secured; finally, since there was no way of avoiding a slight clash in the sixth iambic foot, he frequently tempered the fifth foot by insisting that when it contained a single word, this word must be spondaic. That is, by dwelling upon the first syllable of the fifth foot he reduced the ictus on the second.[17] The result of this exceedingly delicate modulation of the line by Livius—a modulation revealing an astonishingly keen ear—was that the dramatic senarius in

[17] See Lindsay, *Early Latin Verse*, Leo, *Geschichte Lat. Lit.*, p. 68. Fraenkel, *Iktus und Akzent*, seems to me only to have confused the results that have been summarized with consummate skill and good sense by Lindsay.

Latin had a rhythm in which quantitative and accentual beats usually coincided, and this rhythm
served its purpose in Latin drama quite as effectively
as did the trimeter in Greek. Considering the
gentleness of the accent in Latin we may surmise
that Latin dramatic senarii, when thus treated, ran
at least as smoothly as Browning's blank verse
despite the fact that they had to give heed to
accent as well as to quantity.

In teaching the rules of the Latin senarius it is
a pedagogical mistake to compare it with the Greek
trimeter as Lindsay does in his brilliant book, *Early
Latin Verse;* indeed I am persuaded that it distorts
historical facts to do so. If Livius was the man who
shaped this line for Latin needs, we must remember
that he had reached Rome as a mere child and had
as a youth grown accustomed to the swing of verse
pronounced in the Saturnian and the quadratus
meters and that he would not have had any occasion at Rome to learn to comprehend the amazing
precision of the Menandrian trimeter. And Naevius,
the Campanian soldier, must have had much the
same experience. To such men the Greek trimeter
could only have suggested the possibility of writing
a six-foot iambic line which would carry through to
the end, with the lightness of the quadratus, the
opening rhythm of the Saturnian. And the rules
of the first hemistich of the Saturnian must have
been the determining regulations of the senarius.
Those rules had all to do with the purely Latin
problem of writing quantitative verse that should
not overmuch offend the demands of an accentual
stress. Indeed it is fair to say that if Livius had

never seen a Greek trimeter but had undertaken to adapt a six-foot iambic line on suggestions taken only from the Saturnian and the quadratus, he would have arrived at precisely what he did. By failing to see this simple historical sequence we have, from Bentley to the elaborate but misleading statistics of Klotz, followed Horace in misconceiving the spirit of the very worthy Latin senarius.

But there was more for the early dramatists to do than to shape a line suitable for dialogue, for Greek drama had taught these poets that a great variety of meters must be used to give the mood and tempo of emotional scenes. The Roman writers of tragedy did not attempt to reproduce the intricate polymetric and antistrophic Greek songs. However, they adopted several very effective meters (perhaps also creating some) which they used for massed effects, such rhythms as the cretic, bacchiac, anapaestic, glyconic, and the longer iambic and trochaic lines, not to mention various rarer forms. In a fragment of Ennius quoted by Cicero, Andromache in distress runs from senarii through a passage of pleading cretics:

(Quid petam   praesidi aut   exequar   quove nunc
     etc.)

then through excited narration in excellent alliterative septenarii:

(Fana flamma deflagrata tosti alti stant parietes)

into turgid and wild anapaests:

(Priamo vi vitam evitari etc.).

And Cassandra's mad scene runs similarly from septenarii through dactylic tetrameters, trochaic octonarii, and anapaests into iambic octonarii. The tone of such cretics has been caught fairly well in Tennyson's *The Oak*,

> All his leaves, fall'n at length,

while the bacchiac rhythm is, if pronounced with care, conveyed by Arnold's

> Ye storm-winds, of autumn

These brief experiments on the part of English poets, which show an observance of word-stress and also of quantity, will indicate the nature of the difficult task which Latin poetry had to face in taking over meters native to the Greek language, except that the Latin poet, conversely, must place his verse ictus on a long syllable and secondarily, if possible, observe the word stress as well. That was a difficulty with which classical Greek did not have to contend, since its word accent was musical and could easily be slighted. German and English poetry—except in learned experiments—has refused to face the double task, a task which has fortunately never been compulsory.

If we keep these facts in mind I think we may be willing to concede that the Latin poets of the early time may have called in the extended aid of the flute and of melody partly in order to obscure the occasionally inevitable conflict between the word accent and verse ictus. The point can be illustrated by a simple example. In Tennyson's song "Blow, bugle, blow," the line

> And the wild cataract leaps in glory,

which falls unrhythmically in the midst of an iambic system, hides its confusion when sung in regular three-fourths time. The flute or violin, unlike any of the percussion instruments, does not convey a stressing tone, it measures notes and carries a quantitative rhythm readily, thereby obscuring any word accents that fall irregularly.

It is my belief that when the drama came into Rome and found the language just at the point where the quantitative principle was having its conflict for dominance with the accentual factor, a moment when the task of shaping adequate rhythms for new forms would be very difficult, it did the natural thing, accepted quantity as dominant, attempted at the same time to observe the word stress, and then hid occasional discrepancies by using song and recitative freely. And this, it seems to me, is one of the reasons why Roman tragedy was the more willing to go in the direction of modern opera.

If a recent theory concerning French verse be true, we may find there an instructive parallel. It has been suggested that when medieval Latin verse floundered between quantity and accent, early French verse, unable to find usable quantitative distinctions and hampered by a monotonous word accent, hesitated for a dominant principle, and allowed the singing line with its counted notes to assume control. Whether or not this is the reason, at any rate the French lyric emerged with its isosyllabic lines and fluid ictus, and in so far provides a partial parallel to what happened in Latin verse.

It is not improbable that, if the Romans had come in contact with culture a century later than they did, so that the Latin accent might have affected colloquial morphology unhindered by literature and sophistication for another century, native poetry might have abandoned its quantitative basis and frankly accepted word accent as the most vital factor of its rhythm. It would perhaps have been a liberating influence had this happened. As it was, by their use of music and by their reasonable compromise with Greek meters, the early poets accustomed the Roman ear to slight the claims of accent, and Ennius was able to compose spoken lines in hexameters which almost entirely followed the dictates of quantity. Once completely naturalized, this method was no longer questioned, and Lucretius, Horace, and Vergil—except at line ends—could safely disregard the word accents. It was the musical part of the drama that had naturalized such principles of rhythm.

After Accius the writing of tragedy fell off as rapidly at Rome as it had in Greece after the conquests of Alexander. How is this to be explained? Why did not England produce great tragedies after the successes of the Elizabethan stage, or France for a long time after the classical period, or why did not America during the two centuries of playwriting before 1900 beget a single great dramatist? Recently there was published a list of the American plays copyrighted in Washington between 1870 and 1920; it contains over 60,000 titles. How many of these have become a part of the world's literature? Probably not one in 10,000. Can we explain why?

It is not well to be dogmatic in discussing the reasons for such a phenomenon as the decline of tragedy at Rome, but we may be permitted perhaps to repeat some conjectures. We have already remarked[18] that the second century B.C. was a period of striking social changes, of a decrease in the middle class native stock and a very remarkable increase in the slave population, and from this slave population there grew up at Rome the new generation of proletariat citizens that had to be amused at festival seasons. It was a population that was probably as intelligent as the old, but it had hitherto been brought up in slavery and in the devotion to material advancement that slavery implies. These new Romans could hardly be expected to concern themselves with the quality of the entertainment provided, with civic ideals and artistic standards. In Cicero's day the games at festivals were more frequently gladiatorial shows and wild beast hunts. To freedmen and freedmen's sons these seemed to provide what Aristotle called tragic purgation somewhat more effectively than did representations of the *Medea*, *Orestes*, and *Oedipus*. It is apparent that if society was to continue in its course of degeneration the exacting tragedy·of the old type was doomed.

Nevertheless, the old plays were being revived by men who were interested in high standards, and when a famous actor played a part he would draw large audiences. Aesopus and Roscius, the best actors of Cicero's day, were in great demand and both grew rich at their profession. Though refer-

18 In chap. I.

ences to dramatic performances in Cicero's day are casual, we hear of not a few. We know, for instance, that there were reproductions of Ennius' plays a century after his death, and we find in the list his *Andromache*, *Telamo*, *Thyestes*, the *Alcumeo*, the *Iphigenia* and the *Hector*. Of Pacuvius' plays Cicero had seen the *Antiope*, the *Iliona*, and a play about Orestes which he describes as a favorite of the gallery. Accius was even more popular. Aesopus produced his *Atreus* repeatedly. His *Eurysaces* was given in 57 B.C., the *Clytemestra* in 55, and the *Tereus* in 44 after the authorities had suppressed the *Brutus* because of its political significance. And there were many more.

This success of the old plays—artificial though it may have been in some instances—shows that respectable audiences could still be reckoned on so long as the Republic lasted, and that the plays were attractive enough to justify the aediles in presenting them. With the Empire, however, the decline was rapid; the populace found the tragedies tedious, and when in Horace's day a popular actor discovered a way of cutting the plays and presenting the more effective scenes in pantomime, with a lavish amount of music and a gorgeous setting, legitimate tragedy gave way to something resembling a Russian ballet. Old tragedies were cut and adapted for this new kind of presentation and new ones were written that consisted chiefly of scenarios and monologues. Even closet plays, like Seneca's, were shaped into a succession of recitations in the hope that they might sell to the new industry. Literary tragedy, however, had come to its end at Rome.

This process of decay was natural enough and was only to be expected, given the changes in Rome's society and with them the decline of Roman ideals. But it is still somewhat of a riddle why at Rome as well as at Athens good playwrights ceased to write a hundred years before tragedy ceased to attract respectable audiences. It would seem as if the art of writing plays lost its stimulus even before the plays themselves ceased to please. The reason for this may well be that tragedy kept too long to its convention of interpreting sacred myths. The themes were outworn, and each myth had had every human interest exploited by the time that several writers had given it their several interpretations.

Today it would seem quite the obvious thing to have dramatized fictitious experience, even as comedy had long ago learned to do. But a moment's reflection will show that to assume that this might have been done involves an anachronism. Greece did not take this step after Euripides, for Agathon's experiment was not followed, nor France for some time after the classical period, nor England after the Elizabethan successes, and conditions at Rome in the days of Accius were in many respects analogous to those in the countries named. Though the dramatic instinct seems always to be presumable, the drama depends upon social conditions and must draw its life from that which society provides. Its evolution has accordingly been a fairly consistent story. Early tragedy assumes the rôle of interpreting the most sacred and time-honored of a nation's stories. The sufferings, thoughts, emotions of the great—heroes, demigods, and kings—are

worthy of presentation, and these alone. At first
the tale must not be altered, it must be told as
nearly as possible in the way that tradition has
hallowed. As time goes on, however, and men have
changed, the tale thus told will seem inconsonant
with human nature; then the dramatist may re-tell
it, suppressing what has grown obsolete, emphasizing the elements that still seem true to experience.
A very daring realist will venture to present Tele-
phus in tatters, but the critics will be upon his heels
immediately. For the hero will remind you of a
beggar, and it would be desecration to set mere man
upon the stage made for the demigods. Common
man belongs in comedy; you may laugh at him and
with him, but life's great lessons are illustrated only
in the characters of the great. And that is where
Euripides stopped—was doubtless compelled to
stop. And it is nearly where Shakespeare found the
outward boundary of his tragedies. His tragic plots
derive from old Chronicles or from Ancient Rome,
or from foreign lands sufficiently removed from his
audience by mists of unknown space to make them
suitably heroic. His tragic characters never represent the men of contemporary England. They are
as real and human as the man of the street, to be
sure; but that is after all not the same thing. Try
to imagine the heroines of Ibsen or Pinero or O'Neill
upon the stage of the Globe Theatre in Shakespeare's day! The Elizabethan conception of the
function of tragedy makes such heroines unthinkable
except in comic rôles.

Realistic tragedy is of course a thing of slow
growth, or perhaps we should say that a nation fits

itself slowly for the reception of it. Comedy paves the way somewhat. When the great may not be laughed at, it is well that comedy should present the foibles and deformities of the common man, if it be merely for ridicule. Slaves served the purpose of comedy for Menander and Plautus, though they were careful not to compromise the dignity of their art by giving title rôles to such humble fellows. Yet as a matter of fact the study of mean subjects contributed directly and very largely to the understanding of the ordinary character as material for tragedy. Shakespeare's portraiture of Shylock, for example, carried him so far that modern critics do not know where comedy ends and tragedy begins. In the *Andria*, the *Hecyra*, and the *Heauton* of Terence the emotion shifts more than once from laughter to deep sympathy. But something more was needed than the dramatist's study of the man of the street. Human society must itself change. It is not an accident that genuine realistic tragedy failed to find its fully accepted place upon the stage till the nineteenth century, in a word not till thoroughgoing democracy, by preaching the equality of men, had persuaded us of the dignity of the mere human being, and through the prose novel taught the man on the street to concern himself with his fellows as worthy themes of art. That was a stage of democratic realism which Rome did not reach while the literary art was still creative. And therein probably lies the final explanation of the slow failure of Roman tragedy.

CHAPTER III

GREEK COMEDY ON THE ROMAN STAGE

The theme of Roman *gravitas* has perhaps been overworked. The impression seems to be current that Roman schoolboys cheered at the ball games in periodic sentences, and that Roman babes begged for the moon in quantitative hexameters. It appears to be difficult to imagine that the Romans took a very special pleasure in rollicking comedy. Only twenty-six of their comedies have survived, but it is safe to say that if we now had all the respectable literature of the period before 100 B.C., including the epics, the tragedies, the minor verse, and even the artistic prose, the shelves that held the comedies would easily outnumber all the rest. Of what other nation is that true? We have the titles of over four hundred of these plays for the Republican period and there is no reason to suppose that we have even an approach to the full list.

As we have said, the Romans, like all the peoples who followed the Greeks, had to take cognizance of what had been done before. Livius and Naevius were the first to adapt Greek comedies for the Roman stage, as they had been the first to adapt Greek tragedies. Of their work, however, we have again only fragments, saved usually by late grammarians to illustrate archaic grammar. Of Naevius we know the titles of thirty-four comedies, an average of one a year during his period of activity—but since many of these have come to us by the merest coincidence we should not assume that we know all the names of his comedies by any means. Most of these thirty-four plays were adapted from the Greek, but not all. The man who wrote the first Roman epic and the first Roman chronicle play (praetexta) was probably never a slavish copyist. We have noticed how he came to grief for his daring in attacking the powerful Metelli during a critical period of the war. Such criticism would presumably appear in Roman plays. The fragments of his comedies also show many local references that are best explained as coming from plays purely Roman, and such titles as *Hariolus*, *Tunicularia*, and *Agitatoria* suggest independent work. However, so long as we have only about a hundred complete lines rescued from all the plays we can hardly speak with certainty on this point.

In discussing tragedy we suggested that Livius and Naevius were probably the men who shaped the "operatic" form of Roman tragedy, and it is likely that they too were the men who carried this form into comedy, though its final development seems to be due to Plautus. The distinctly lyric lines are rare, to be sure, but the fragments are too few to permit us to expect many. The majority are iambic, the Roman equivalent of the Greek originals, and they have of course the free Latin form. One line is anapaestic; the old Roman trochaic septenarius, well suited to song, is frequent and so is the iambic octonarius, which Naevius seems to treat like a septenarius with anacrusis. Indeed Cicero[1] calls it a septenarius and indicates that it was sung to the accompaniment of the flute.

These were the comedies which entertained the Romans at their festivals during the gloomy years of the Punic war, those years that are so vividly pictured for us by Livy. If we could recover these plays and interpolate them between the harrowing scenes of Livy's history we should know more than we do of Roman society during that most critical epoch of the nation's history.

Plautus, from whom we have twenty plays, had staged a few of them before Naevius went into exile, in fact in the *Miles Gloriosus* he refers to the imprisonment of his fellow-poet. In his plots Plautus kept rather close to the Greek plays, translating, paraphrasing, and adapting as suited his mood. We shall presently discuss his reasons for doing so. What these themes were we need not repeat. The Greeks of Menander's day had shaped the comedies of intrigue and of romance fairly well on the lines these have followed ever since. Shakespeare's *Comedy of Errors* is very close to Plautus' *Menaechmi*, and though it departs from its original in its search for further entanglements, the construction, the type of humor, and the dramatic devices are the same. In the *Merry Wives of Windsor*, Falstaff illustrates the Menandrian use of self-deception, from his first boasting to his leap into the basket. The Wives are more in evidence than they would have been in Menander but there is little else to distinguish the play from the standard New Comedy.

[1] Cic. *Tusc.* i. 106–7.

From the Greek, via Plautus and Terence, came practically all the types and all the tricks in which Elizabethan and Jacobean comedy delighted.

Here it is my task not to discuss Roman comedy as such, but rather to indicate what in Rome's life and experiences made itself felt through these plays. In the Plautine adaptations of Greek comedies we find two seemingly inconsistent purposes, one to rewrite in such a way as to make the exotic comprehensible, the other to keep a Greek atmosphere in order not to offend Roman taste by permitting the inference that the author approved of the behavior which he presented. The first purpose required simplification, the second avoided it. It is necessary to dwell upon this distinction for a moment since historians frequently fall into error by assuming either that Plautus reproduced a Greek milieu without alteration or on the contrary that he represented Roman life as he found it. In point of fact he did both or either, as best suited his purpose.

In technicalities of law, to take a simple illustration, Plautus' procedure was to simplify with little regard for consistency. At times when it did not matter he substituted Roman officials or institutions for Greek ones without concern as to whether they were exact equivalents. If in presenting the details of a lawsuit a literal translation of the Greek would seem obscure to a Roman audience, Plautus substituted some comprehensible point and reshaped the whole passage to conform to his illustration. In short, he used mere common sense in adapting foreign plays for stage production. Had Plautus been translating for a reading public he might have given a literal rendering and inserted a note of explanation. But plays written for a single presentation have no occasion for employing explanatory notes.

Scholars have also been troubled by the fact that the plays of Plautus bristle with Greek words. There is an average of about ninety occurrences a play, counting repetitions of the same word. How would our comedies fare on the stage if foreign words were used with equal lavishness? Not a few of these words—like *amphora, ancora, epistula*—had of course been acclimated through commerce, and would cause no trouble. A few technical names that could not be translated—of Greek magistrates, for instance—were illumined by the context. In a few instances Plautus literally dumps in Greek words for amusement, as when an irate husband reels off the items of the bill he has received from the modiste, or reads the menu that will cost him more than he is able to pay. Such words the audience were hardly expected to know. The very outlandish extravagance of the list is intentional. But after we have made these subtractions, the bulk remains.[2] Are we to assume that Plautus addressed his plays to the score of cultured gentlemen who had had Greek tutors? If he had, the aediles would hardly have gone to the expense of buying the plays and presenting them, for the purpose of the games was to attract and amuse the holiday masses. Can it be that Plautus indolently neglected to invent Latin

[2] Leo, *Plautinische Forschungen*, 106; Fraenkel, *Plautinisches im Plautus*, 157; Kahle, *De Vocabulis Graecis Plauti aetate:* and Hoffmann, *in* Stoltz-Schmalz, p. 813, have made some interesting observations regarding the use of Greek words in Plautus but have failed to note the pertinent historical facts.

jokes in place of the Greek ones of his models?
That is hardly a satisfactory solution in the case
of a writer who inundates his scenes with rollicking
fun. Another common explanation—too frequently
hazarded—that the streets were already overrun
with Greek captives who had spread a knowledge
of Greek, will hardly serve. In neither of the Punic
wars had many Greek captives been taken—the
captives had been chiefly Carthaginian, and their
Spanish, Gallic, and Ligurian mercenaries—and
these are not noticed in the Plautine plays.[3]

The simple explanation is that most of the
Roman populace had served in many campaigns in
Greek cities and with Greek contingents and had
become familiar with a great number of colloquial
Greek expressions, in the same way that American
boys acquired not a few French phrases some years
ago in their one brief campaign overseas. The older
generation had served in Sicily in the First Punic
War and had been billeted in Greek towns for
periods of from six to twelve years. The younger
men had all served in the Greek districts of southern
Italy before Hannibal was finally driven out in
203 B.C. Both of these wars strained Rome's man
power to the very limit so that practically every
adult male saw service in Greek-speaking communities. And finally, during the last years of Plautus'
activity, a dozen legions were sent across the Adri-
atic for the campaigns against Philip and Antiochus.
Plautus could probably assume therefore that at

[3] The greeting *ave* is a curious instance of borrowing from the
Punic. The word was perhaps brought back by the soldiers from their
camps in the Punic parts of Sicily. The Romans had besieged the
Punic forts of Lilybaeum for eight years.

least ninety per cent of the able-bodied men of his audience had served in campaigns among and with Greeks. Those retired soldiers were happy to be complimented with reminders of their services to the state, and Plautus did it by frequent references to the language they had acquired in the wars.[4]

The liberal use of military terms like *machaera*,[5] *ballista*, *catapulta*, *phylaca*, *techina*, *machina*, even in all kinds of figurative senses; of exclamations and terms of abuse that the soldiers would hear when out prowling for extra rations: *barbarus*, *harpago*, *dierecte*, *latro*, *morus*, *plaga*, *colapus*, *mastigia*, *ganeum* *gerrae*, *apage*, *pax*, *papae*, *babae*, *eia*, *eugepae*, and the rest; of canteen phrases convenient on pay-days in Sicily: *drachuma*, *danista*, *trapezita*, *opsonium*, *cyathisso*, *crapula*, *oenopolium*, *macellum*, *comissatum*

---

[4] Plautus likes to address the soldiers of his audiences, cf. *Capt.* 68; *Cist.* 197; *Cas.* 87; etc.

[5] It is difficult to say when the great vowel-shift took place in Latin. It is clear that Greek words in Plautus like *calamus*, *colaphus*, and *hilarus* had not come under the influence of the shift. Either they were very recent arrivals or had been used so little in Latin folk-speech (like *barbarus*, a Greek term of abuse) that Plautus could spell them in the Greek fashion. Words like *oliva*, *Hercules*, *Massilia*, *Tarentum* were of course acclimated long before and took on the regular vowel changes of Latin. However it is probable that many Greek words that were adopted during the Pyrrhic and first Punic wars felt the full influence of the great shift. This shift seems to have begun after the twelve tables and the Duenos inscription and it was by no means over when Plautus wrote: cf. the inscriptional spelling *mereto*, *soledas*, *Esquelino*, *Arimenese*, *popolom*, *saxolus*, etc. It is difficult to see how *Acragas* (Agrigentum) could have got into frequent Latin usage before 262 B.C. It is highly probable that the vowel-shift in Latin, like the similar change in English, marks a politico-social shift, an emergence of a social group that pronounced certain vowels in a way not considered correct in aristocratic Rome. We may possibly associate it with the elevation of the plebeians after the Publilian and Hortensian laws of 339 and 287 B.C., which made the tribal assembly supreme in Roman legislation. The new tendencies in pronunciation would then be a strong factor in speech during the First Punic War. Furthermore, the fact that the dramatists could transform Δήμοφων to Demipho at one stroke shows how quickly a word would adapt itself to Latin custom. I feel sure that we have placed the arrival of most of the Greek words too early.

eo (and shall we add *gynaeceum?*), this tells an unmistakable story. A large number of these expressions were little used at Rome after the period of general campaigning among the Greeks. Many point directly to Sicily. The word *lautumiae*, for example, reminds us of the convict quarries of Syracuse, *basilike* ("right royally") seems to betray the soldiers' respect for the lavish court of King Hiero, as *Siculi logi* reflects their impression of a talkative people. A large number of the words are Doric in formation, deriving apparently from Sicily or Tarentum: *choragus* (used in an un-Attic sense and sound), *plaga, machina, zamia, catapulta,*[6] *colapus, ganeum, gerrae, sumbola,* and many others. Not a few words were demonstrably adopted by speakers rather than by writers, as *phylaca, gerrae, balineum, lanterna,* etc.

This is but a brief indication of the linguistic evidence that the soldiers returned home with a convenient Greek vocabulary of no small scope. How freely Plautus could assume its ready use is revealed by his lavishness in compounding such Greek words with Latin termination as in *athletice, dulice, euscheme, inanilogista, morologus, pultiphagus, pancratice, opsonari, plagipatidae, elleborosus, ulmi-*

---

[6] *Catapulta* was probably not very old in Latin since only the third syllable shows a change, and that a relatively late one. In words like *sumbola* we doubtless have the Doric pronunciation of *v*; in the short penult of *gynaeceum, balinea,* and *platea,* the cause need not lie wholly in a Latin tendency to shorten one vowel before another but in part perhaps to the similar tendency found in Greek and especially in Sicilian. In Latin *latro, barbarus, choragus,* and the like we certainly have not standard Greek meanings but such as might have been heard in Sicily during the Punic war. Sturtevant's interesting discussion "Concerning the Use of Greek in Vulgar Latin," *Trans. Am. Phil. Assoc.* (1925), quite misses the heart of the question when it speaks of the "Romans consciously mocking the Greeks of the city." There were very few Greeks there then, and they were not significant enough to invite mocking.

triba, and even in the use of Greek oaths (μὰ τὸν 'Απόλλων) of semi-Greek puns (*opus est chryso Chrysalo*, etc.), and Greek slang (*argentum* οἴχεται). But we may be sure that Plautus knew very well the precise limits of this camp language. He does not venture to employ the common colloquialisms of the literary Greek of Menander if they are not a part of the military store of his day. For those he finds Latin substitutes. Very likely Plautus had himself served as a soldier in southern Italy during the Hannibalic war and had there acquired an accurate knowledge of the diction that could be intelligible to his audience of soldier folk.

There has also been much speculation concerning Plautus' relatively free use of Greek mythology, since the sophisticated new Greek comedy rather avoided any reference to it.[7] In the *Bacchides* of Plautus the clever slave compares his exploits in detail with the devices used in the capture of Troy (the theft of the Palladium and the building of the Trojan horse); in the *Rudens*, Charmides promises a "feast of Thyestes"; in the *Captives*, Tyndarus refers familiarly to Orestes and Lycurgus; everywhere the names of Achilles, Hector, Medea, and the like are spoken of as well known. This cannot be explained by recalling that the Odyssey had been translated into Latin, since reading was by no means general, nor by pointing to the use of these myths for illustrations on Etruscan vases and mirrors. Not one in a thousand of the auditors had come into contact with Homer or with such objects of art. But the

---

[7] Fraenkel, *Plautinisches im Plautus*, chap. III; unfortunately he has failed to comprehend the nature of the Plautine public. Legrand's *Daos* makes the more serious mistake of treating the Greek and Roman New Comedy as a single phenomenon.

crowds for whom Plautus wrote had for thirty years had free seats on the holidays when the tragedies of Livius, Naevius, and Ennius were played, and they knew the characters of those tragedies as well as the laboring men of today know the names of our baseball pitchers and cinema stars.

The Trojan cycle was particularly familiar from the theater because the dramatists, exploiting the tradition that the Romans were descendants of the Trojans, had presented all the good plays that they could find on this theme. Livius had produced an *Equus Trojanus*, an *Achilles*, an *Aegisthus*, and an *Ajax*, which must have told of every phase of the subject, and the Livian *Hermione* had familiarized them with some of the aftermath of the war. Plautus' ready mention of Procne and Philomela is readily explained by recalling that Livius had presented the *Tereus*. The impression made by the Trojan cycle of Livius had been deepened by the several plays written on these myths by Naevius; the *Hesione*, *Iphigenia*, *Hector*, *Equus Trojanus*, and *Andromache* all dealt with characters of the Trojan cycle, while the *Danae* and the *Lycurgus* supplied adjacent myths that the Plautine audiences evidently knew. These plays—and of course there were many whose names have been lost—would account for most of the familiar references in Plautus. Furthermore, Ennius was producing tragedies at the very festivals for which Plautus wrote, and here and there we can actually recognize in Plautus certain lines that were spoken as parodies of Ennian lines.[8] We do not know the chronology of the plays of these dramatists. If we could syn-

[8] Sedgwick, *Class. Quart.* 1927, 88.

chronize them now we should probably find that the references to Andromeda, Alcumeo, Thyestes, and other characters of the Greek myths would fall in neatly with plays of Ennius on these themes which had been recently produced.

It is quite beside the point to ask how much "literature" the Plautine audience knew. They knew no literature as such, but they all attended the festival shows which were free. There they learned the stories of a large number of the plays of Euripides and Sophocles as easily as our working classes learn, without opening a book, about Arab sheikhs, Long Island drawing rooms, Roman chariot races, and Cleopatra's wiles. To them in fact a play of Euripides was often the latest popular sensation.

Many years ago when Max Reinhardt first staged *Oedipus* in the Circus at Berlin at prices that attracted hundreds of laboring men I overheard these remarks: "This Sophocles, is he a Berliner?" "I don't know; the name sounds Russian; but he knows how to make a good show." Those two men had enjoyed the play all the more because they did not know they were being educated in the ancient classics; and that is how Plautus' audience had innocently learned its Greek mythology. Naturally Plautus was too wise not to exploit this rich vein of interest.

So thoroughly un-Greek is Plautus in his type of rollicking humor, in his volubility, in his skurrying speed, and in his love for exciting intrigue—if we may assume that the recently discovered plays of Menander are typical of the Greek New Comedy— that we are surprised at his refusal to write original and purely Roman comedies. He invariably keeps the scene in Greece, dresses his characters in Greek garb, and gives them Greek names. What is the reason? Naevius had written plays on Roman themes. Why did not Plautus? That it was diffidence one can hardly believe after noting the originality he displayed in adapting the plays to musical settings and the success he achieved in writing the scenes that are demonstrably his.

The secret of Plautus' behavior in this matter seems to me to lie in his appreciation of the fact that Rome was still too conservative to accept as Roman the intrigues and plots that would make the richest comedy. "Spoon River," as we have learned, has its vices, but at Spoon River they are studiously hidden under a cloak of Sunday respectability. When a modern playwright wishes to add more piquancy to a play than an American milieu will unprotestingly support he lays his scene in Paris or on a South Sea island. There is enough human nature under the frown—or smile—to comprehend what is presented, and sins can be the more openly discussed and condemned—or laughed at—if the spectator is permitted at the same time to express his puritanic superiority to the mores of an exotic society admittedly going to its deserved ruin. This seems to be the reason why Plautus lets his amusingly extravagant slaves, demi-mondaines, and reckless young men play freely with moral values in a Greek setting, usually with an explicit condemnation of the villain at the end, and often with a reminder that "such things are possible at Athens."[9] The characters of Plautus, therefore, are never

[9] *Stich.* 448, *licet haec Athenis nobis: Men.* 7–9.   At the end of the *Bacchides* Plautus becomes very apologetic for the immoral last scene.

Roman in outward appearance, and it is a mistake to assume that Roman manners are depicted in his plays, even if here and there he is compelled to take cognizance of Roman morals.

The spendthrift young men with the resourceful slaves who help them to their desires by concocting astute schemes are Greek. The Athens of Menander was sophisticated. There clever young men had penetrated beyond Epicurus' ethical sophistry to the logical naturalism of his premises; they had even waved aside the forced idealistic definition of "nature" which Zeno was teaching them to follow and had learned to give allegiance to a simpler nature more responsive to immediate wishes. Pristine authority, filial respect, and the compulsion of academic ethics were all weakened by the prevalent discovery that no system of faith as yet invented had withstood penetrating criticism. Young men saw no valid objection in logic to doing as they liked. And many were in a position to do as they liked, since theirs was the generation for which Alexander had ransacked the treasures of the east, opened lucrative commerce to shrewd traders, sent hordes of cheap slaves to do the hard work of a civilized world, and caravans of music girls, dancers, and courtesans to entertain a sophisticated city. The *jeunesse dorée* of Athens, pleasure-loving, undisciplined, helplessly inexperienced, epicures living to the ragged edge of incomes and beyond, were fit subjects for a comedy whose god was luck. They were not yet brutalized, they usually had a gentlemanly code of a kind, and they were often generously devoted humans. But they had no anchorage in principles. Such were the young men in Menander, and such Plautus, who had an eye for color, preferred to keep them, despite their non-Roman aspect. But he was very careful to keep them Greek.

At Rome at the end of the great Punic war a young man's life was a very different matter. For nearly twenty years the dreadful scourge of Punic raids had impoverished the people. Every ablebodied man of military age was in the trenches living on the most frugal fare; farms were mortgaged and lying waste; war taxes were growing; the state was pressing down with sumptuary laws that forbade luxury, limiting clothing to homespun, and food to a few cents a day. And even when the Punic war was over, the aftermath of campaigns against the rebellious Gauls, against Spain and Macedonia gave no respite till near the end of Plautus' life. Doubtless the young men, who could see the Plautine plays on the three or four holidays each year when they were given, enjoyed vicariously a release of spirit which they could comprehend because they were human beings. But not one of them had actually lived at home in the atmosphere reproduced on the Plautine stage. It is not surprising, therefore, that Plautus kept the Greek setting. There was little to draw upon from Roman life. Had he put his people in Roman dress the incongruity would have been ludicrous; and the censors would have realized the danger to morality and suppressed the plays. As exotic myths they seemed less harmful—though the time was to come and sooner than could have been expected when the characters of these plays were to take on a semblance of realism even at Rome.

What is true of Plautus' young *roués* is also true of the Plautine parasites and slaves. The amusing parasites, the Athenian wits who got their bread by providing entertaining talk, were as useful in the New Comedy as are the futile expatriate artists in the modern international novel, but there is no evidence that these creatures had as yet made their way to Rome. The Plautine slave is a mixed character. It has been customary to say that Rome's culture depended more heavily on slavery than Greece's and that therefore the comic slave is Plautine rather than Greek. But that assumption disregards a century of economic change. The slave of comedy usually is a very clever rascal, very loyal to his young master for whose least pleasure he will trick parents and police; he is amazingly resourceful, quick of wit, possessed of a sauciness that we cannot associate with early Roman custom, and capable of enduring blows if he has a good conscience from having successfully perpetrated his crimes. In sophisticated Athens this character is wholly plausible; at Rome in the day of Plautus he is not. It is true that Menander's fragments use slaves less than the Plautine plays; this probably means that Plautus, in following some of the dramatists of the New Comedy, avoided Menandrian plays because they had not enough boisterous fun for him per page. It does not mean that Plautus in this respect is closer to Roman life. We used to be told also that scenes of slave torture in comedy were purely Roman, but we now have a scene in Menander's

Perinthia which goes so far in cruelty that Terence omitted this scene. Here again, therefore, we have not a Roman characteristic. The fact is that in Plautus' day slaves were relatively scarce at Rome; the working classes in the city were still largely free natives, the farms were usually owned in small plots by working farmers, and the few slaves on them were still treated in the way that single farm hands are usually treated in our own simpler rural districts, that is, as members of the household. Bound slaves were very rare, the *ergastulum* was hardly known as yet, and the slave when set free still became a citizen with the same status as his master. It was not till the end of the Punic war that Rome for the first time knew what it was to possess non-Italic captives in considerable numbers—slaves who had to be bound and watched—and of course it required a generation or two of slave culture on large villas and estates before the saucy type could appear, the type familiar to us in the comedies. No, this type would perhaps be plausible at Rome in the Gracchan day, but not before. My feeling is that Plautus has not only given us the Greek type as he found it, but, since the morality of citizens was not involved in a slave's rascalities, he has somewhat padded his plays with slave intrigue in order to speed up his action. Not from a single trait should we infer that he depicted the Roman slave of his own day. It is significant that when true Roman comedies began to be written the slave rôle was at once toned down because, as Donatus says, a Roman master ought not be represented as outwitted by a slave.

In the treatment of female characters Plautus' procedure is somewhat different. Greek New Comedy had a type of woman in the rather respectable hetaerae well adapted to its purpose, and in fact the only type usable, since the Greek housewife was so bound to the dull routine of the rear-of-the-house that she was too devitalized for literary treatment. The metic companion—of Aspasia's station and juristic standing—moved about freely in the city, could be placed in almost any social group, and could by an easy fiction and the proper birth tokens be discovered to be an unrecognized citizen. Since this was the only respectable class available for Menander's intrigues, he naturally employed hetaerae for his many plays that contained love scenes. Roman adapters, however, encountering such heroines, who represented a social class foreign to Roman society, found considerable difficulty in transplanting them to Italian soil. It may be remembered that in the Victorian period the plays of Dumas fils could not readily be transposed into English, just as the romantic English plays of that day failed of comprehension in France, because the relations between the sexes were based on different customs in each country. What, for instance, would Plautus have done on the Roman stage with Habratonon, the shrewd but generously human hetaera of Menander's *Arbitrants*, who, when she had to make her choice, surrendered her own advantages over her lover and restored him to his wife and child? Plautus if he had used such a play would have had to substitute for her a Roman courtesan or else destroy the plot. And if he did employ a

courtesan, Roman realism would have demanded
that she be depicted without generosity, for at
Rome it would not do to let a woman of such a
class seem virtuous. The matrons of Rome would
have objected.[10] In the Roman society of Plautus'
day family relations were puritanic, divorce was
almost unknown, and the Roman matron was her
husband's equal in the home and in society. She
was not relegated to the spinning room in the back
of the house as in Greece; she did not mope in her
chamber while her husband went to dinner parties
and to the theater with his boon companions. She
was the companion. In such a society there may
be and were some "daughters of joy" for pagan
youth, but they were not spoken of, they did not
appear, they were in the dark where generous virtues do not grow. One might suppose that Plautus
could have abandoned the Greek scene, eliminated
the demi-monde, and staged a normal Roman
comedy. But if he were to keep the love story he
would have had to resort to the postmarital triangle
used in such circumstances by the French—a device
unthinkable in the social atmosphere of his day—
or to the romances of free adolescents—a theme not
easily illustrated from the urban life of southern
countries where young girls are carefully cloistered.
In other words, Plautus was very nearly compelled
to choose either to abandon the theme of love-
making in a comic setting, or to adopt the Greek
hetaera; and if he did the latter he was obliged to
deprive her of various pleasant qualities that might

[10] Selenium in the *Cistellaria* and Adelphasium in the *Poenulus* are
favorably portrayed so as not to disappoint the audience when they
are later to be revealed as freeborn.

have been hers in Greece or incur the enmity of Roman moral censorship. Plautus has been severely blamed, especially by French critics, for making his women futile twaddlers with no redeeming features. It is true that this description fits them well enough, but what was he to do? Titinius seems to have found a way out later, but it was not a very obvious way. The method of Plautus should not be ascribed to a coarse grain in the dramatist. It grew naturally from his comprehension of the real status of the Roman family. In adapting Greek slaves, parasites, and young men with little or no change, he might take a risk, but on the subject of Roman womanhood he could not compromise.

It is noticeable that Terence could. Bacchis in the *Hecyra*, who harks back to Habratonon in Menander, has an appealingly generous nature despite her station, and even the morose old man of the play has to admit it. But Terence wrote the *Hecyra* more than twenty years after Plautus' death, at a time when Greek customs had invaded Rome. Today Terence receives the credit for a liberal humanity denied to Plautus, but it is safe to say that Terence would not have ventured to present his Bacchis a generation earlier. His respect for the position and the deserved rights of the women of old Rome would have made him feel that it was a cheap thing to do.

The most striking departure of Roman comedy from the Greek resides in the omission of the choral interludes and the substitution of long lyrical monodies in the place of spoken and recited lines. In the Greek plays the acts were separated by choral interludes, dances, revels, and the like. With the careful costuming as well as with the frequent doubling of rôles in the Greek theater, much time was required for changes of garb. Plautus had few trained singers available for an effective chorus, few dancers, and he needed but little time between the acts, since there was no scene-shifting and masks were not used in his day. A Plautine play was almost a continuous performance, and a performance with an abundance of music. The rapid dialogue that carried the most vital action was usually spoken without musical accompaniment in six-foot iambics. This dialogue usually constituted about a third of the play. Soliloquies, monologues (except in prologues), and scenes of tense emotion were apt to be sung to the flute in a variety of meters that kept changing to suit the mood and the emotion. These parts, called *cantica*, were rare in some plays and especially in the early ones, while in others they took up as much as a third of the play. To these cantica we shall presently return. Certain scenes composed of recitative were accompanied by the flute. Such scenes we are accustomed to even now, especially in sentimental plays where love-making and moonlight are signals for the muted violins to accompany the spoken words with a soft obligato. In Plautus the meters of such scenes, usually seven- and eight-foot lines, vary considerably from the normal dialogue verse.

There is only one passage in ancient comedy in which we happen to have the original Greek material re-cast into a Roman canticum. A late critic, Aulus Gellius,[11] quotes a song of Caecilius, and with

[11] A. Gellius, II, 23, 6.

it the original Greek to demonstrate what he calls
the inadequacy of the Latin paraphrase. Gellius,
however, misses the point. The substance of the
Greek—the conventional complaints of a scold-
ridden husband—was deliberately changed. The
smooth narration of the original was not suited to
song, and Caecilius wanted a text that would give
the musician a chance to bring out effectively the
constantly changing emotions of the speaker. In
the Greek the husband simply informs the audience,
with suitable comment, that his wife, jealous of her
slave maid, has had her sold to get her out of the
house. There is of course no great depth to the
husband's emotions, though the range from pity to
sarcasm is well enough brought out. The Latin
version stresses this variation of mood by a constant
shift of meters, the verse running speedily from the
tripping trochaic septenarii through cretics, bacchiacs, cretics again, and then iambics. The man
comes on shouting to music that changes its rhythm
with every line.

> (— ∪) Always scolding, nagging, dinning she com-
> pelled me to obey:
> (— ∪ —) Innocence goes for naught: the maid is sold.
> (∪ — —) Now gloating and boasting my good wife
> appears:
> (— ∪ —) Tell me pray, what am I? Who is master
> here?

The point made by the ancient critic that Caecilius
did not adequately reproduce the original quality
is wholly beside the point. He was not attempting
to. He was making a plausible libretto for a brief
song and dance in which melody, pitch, tempo, and
gesture should aid in the expression of his varying

moods. Menander indeed had written a readable play—he always did, and paid the penalty by seldom taking the prize. But Caecilius produced a musical comedy which, it is safe to wager, kept the audience physically responsive.

It has been usual to suppose that Plautus invented the musical comedy of this type.[12] I have already referred to Naevius' introduction of the canticum into tragedy. It had the same function in comedy and I need only repeat that Naevius served in Sicily as a soldier in the First Punic War, and that in many of the Greek towns of Sicily where the Roman soldiers were billeted, or at least resorted on furloughs, Greek tragedies and comedies were being produced in the theaters, probably with reduced choruses.[13] That is where Naevius may have found his model of the canticum. It should also be remembered that a great variety of what may be called music-hall singing and dancing went on in such places at that time. If the Roman soldiers grew fond of such performances, it would not be surprising if Naevius tried to supply in his comedies as well as in his tragedies some substitute for what Rome did not have. Audiences may make insistent demands: even Wagner was compelled to insert ballets in his operas in order to satisfy the demands of his Parisian audiences. The fragments from Naevius' comedies

[12] Leo, *Plaut. Cantica*: Fraenkel, *op. cit.*, chap. X, who, however, draws upon Ennius more than the dates permit. The so-called epitaph of Plautus apparently credited him with special praise for his elaborate songs (*numeri innumeri*).

[13] There were theaters at least in Syracuse, Tauromenium, Segesta (the seat of a Roman garrison throughout the period of the war), Agyrion, Tyndaris, Akrae, and Catania; see Bieber, *Denkmäler d. Theaterwesen*, 50. *Choragus* is a Doric form that might readily have come from Segesta.

are few, and in them there are none of the purely
lyrical meters so often found in Plautus—the cretics, the bacchiacs, and the glyconics. But there is
a large proportion of trochaic septenarii, lines which
are now assumed to belong to a native Latin song
meter.[14] Our evidence is slight as yet but it is perhaps sufficient to support a suggestion that musical
comedy may have grown up at Rome through the
gradual adaptation of Sicilian forms of entertainment by Naevius and a constant improvement upon
these innovations by Plautus. We have also seen
that song and chant were a decided aid in the
attempt to accommodate new meters to the Roman
ear.

In observing how literature may be determined
by externals we must not omit to notice certain
customs of staging that affected the plays. The
Roman *ludi*, at which the plays were first given,
had formerly been devoted chiefly to chariot races.
These races seem to have come in at first when,
before and after campaigns, the army was purified.
The knights and charioteers took part in the lus-
tration and used the occasion to demonstrate the
skill of their horses. At the *Ludi Romani*, held in
September, which grew out of triumphal processions
to Jupiter's temple, the races were probably not
considered in historical times as having any religious
associations. They were held for purposes of entertainment, and the plays, the *ludi scaenici*, which
were added to the races in 240 B.C., were also given
for entertainment and had in themselves none of the
sacred associations so persistently connected with
the Greek performances.

[14] Cf. Fraenkel on the "Versus quadratus," *Hermes*, 1927, 357.

Now these Roman games were directed by the magistrates, who used for them an appropriation granted by the state, an appropriation, however, which seldom covered the costs. The Senate in fact took advantage of the knowledge that men who had reached the aedileship by popular favor were likely to entertain the people well in order to hold that favor at the next election. Obviously the aediles who paid the costs would choose plays of a nature to please the average Roman citizen. In saying the average Roman we mean that most of the men and women of the middle and lower classes would expect to see the plays. Scipio, to be sure, tried to attract the nobility by setting apart the first rows for them, and he probably succeeded to some extent, at least when good tragedies were given, if we may judge from Cicero's familiarity with the acting of Aesopus. However, had the majority of the senatorial nobles been enthusiastic attendants, Rome would not have had to wait nearly two centuries for a permanent theater. We must assume for most performances a crowd of holiday idlers from the streets and shops who looked for something at least as interesting as tippling at the bar, and who were quite well aware that the aediles expected defeat at the election if the plays were not satisfactory. We can therefore comprehend why Plautus, who quite regularly succeeded in pleasing his audience, packed a great deal more of joking, intrigue, and broad humor into his plays than did Menander, for instance; why his plots are simpler, reveal less characterization, and in general concern themselves less with the artistic unfolding of a story than Menander's and, finally, why the song and dance scenes constantly increase in number in the late Plautine plays.

Conversely, when we think of the audience, and then compare these plays with the cinema shows sometimes given to entice crowds of voters to political gatherings, we can only be surprised at the relatively high grade of entertainment that the Roman comedies contain. Rome's holiday crowds in Plautus' day consisted of plain folk, but they must have been intelligent and unspoiled. The mimes and farces of a century later certainly reflect a decided deterioration in the theater-goers of that time. Horace was not entirely fair when he accused Plautus of writing down for the sake of filling his purse. Perhaps he did, but after all he did not stoop to the kind of audiences that later entertainers amused for profit. Horace in fact should have compared Plautus with Laberius and Publilius and not, as he did, with the nicer closet drama of his own day which never had a chance of being produced.

We may also recall that Plautus wrote for a single performance with no thought of publication, of a reading public or even of a revival of the play. He sold his manuscript and after the play was over the manuscript was placed in the state archives, perhaps never to be seen again. Plautus of course did not know that many of the plays would be dug up for reproduction a generation later when there was a dearth of good writers. We shall also do well to remember that there were no programs distributed at the performances. These circumstances account for the dramatist's endeavor to make his plays self-explanatory and self-contained, for his willingness to continue the old convention of revealing the plot early, to keep its progress clear and explicit, to get immediate effects and not to concern himself too much as to whether an effective scene at the end is entirely consistent with the implications at the beginning. The spectator could not refer to a published copy, nor return next day to examine the play critically. Most scholarly guessing as to whether blemishes may have crept into these plays by successive revisions is based upon a minute analysis of them in the study, the very kind of analysis that Plautus never expected to receive. Plautus counted to a certain extent on the auditor's capacity to forget as well as on his ability to remember. One curious result of this habit of presenting a new play at each festival was that a great many plays accumulated in the archives, and so when, in the time of Terence, officials began to resurrect old plays, the available stock glutted the market. At that time the authors of new plays must actually have been hurt by the competition of dead authors.

One of the greatest difficulties that the dramatists had to contend with in the old day was the securing of good actors. Not only did Livius begin without the aid of any trained actors, but for half a century at least the profession was not attractive. Livius seems to have formed his own troupe. Naevius may have depended somewhat on players from Campania who were trained in giving Atellan farces. At least that seems to be the implication of Festus in explaining the term "fabula personata," and we know that Oscan Pompeii had a permanent theater at that time. Polybius, the Greek, found the acting in Roman tragedies very unsatisfactory. The chief difficulty was of course that the games came so rarely that in the early day no actor could possibly have made a living by the profession. For the first twenty years it is likely that at most only two tragedies and two comedies were produced a year at the annual Ludi Romani. In 220 a new festival, the Ludi plebeii, was added for November, but it is not likely that at first plays were given there. At least none are recorded till twenty years later. In 214 the plays were assigned four days of the Ludi Romani, and in 212 games, including plays, were voted in honor of Apollo. Hence we may assume that by the end of the Punic war there would be about six days a year set apart for dramatic performances, that is, about six tragedies and six comedies were played once each year.

Since the aediles (and praetors, in the case of the Apollo games) selected a new play for each performance, the annual offering of plays might be considerable, and some rivalries sprang up among the poets. For instance, a Terentian prologue[15] reveals an amusing situation in which, after the aediles had paid for the play and were inspecting it, a rival dramatist gained admission to the rehearsal and suddenly started to charge Terence with plagiary. In another prologue of Terence, Ambivius, the producer, reminds his audience of how he had in his youth insisted on re-staging rejected plays of Caecilius Statius till the audience learned to like them, adding that Caecilius had

[15] Ter., *Eunuch.* 20 and *Hecyra*, 14.

suffered unjustly from the criticism of rival poets. We may then assume a considerable activity and a not unwholesome rivalry among the dramatists.

But the serious danger to the profession in the early days was the rarity of the productions and the meager opportunity for good actors. Six days of work a year is not apt to create or nourish a specialized profession. Because of the scarcity of actors Livius, presumably Plautus, and also occasionally Atilius, acted in their own plays—as had been the old custom of the poets in Greece. Plautus mentions only one of his actors—Pellio—and says unpleasant things about him. Who the other actors were we do not know. Festus conjectures that Naevius had imported Oscan players for the comedy called *Personata* because of the scarcity of talent. Before the death of Plautus, L. Ambivius Turpio came out as actor-manager for Caecilius, and later we hear of Cincius, a Faliscan, Atilius of Praeneste (perhaps the playwright of that name), and a Minucius. Much later, in the time of Roscius, we know that the scarcity of actors led to the custom of training clever Greek slaves to act, but there is no evidence that slaves were used during the first hundred years of the Roman drama. Very likely the author himself at first took a rôle, brought in Oscan, Greek, and Faliscan actors to some extent, and induced amateurs who made their living by other occupations to help during the festivals. It is quite certain that well into the second century B.C. there were not enough performances to persuade many Romans to enter the profession for a regular living, or to incur the expense of training or keeping slaves for the occupation, as was done later.

We must also take into account the fact that the performances at Rome were not, as in Greece, connected with old and sacred traditions, so that men were not induced to take up the profession because of its glamour and official honors. Plays were introduced at the games purely as an extra entertainment. In Greece where plays had grown up to interpret sacred myths, acting had some religious import so that the state was called upon to give prizes and honors to the profession.

The economic and social factors that we have mentioned account for the fact that Plautus had to continue the Greek habit of doubling rôles even though he did not employ masks, and though he was not bound by any old tradition as to the proper number of actors.[16] Of course the rule of the three actors had broken down even at the time of Euripides, and Menander probably allowed himself five actors at times. Plautus often had ten or twelve characters, but he seems to get along with about four or five actors and in several instances with only three. This accounts for the somewhat artificial excuses that characters are constantly giving for leaving the stage when the actor has to scurry off to dress for a new rôle. Needless to say, this deficiency of actors must have exerted a restraining

[16] Cf. C. M. Kurrelmeyer, *Economy of Actors in Plautus.* The well-known Horatian rule was a later reversion to a Greek rule. Choral singers were apparently imported from Greece in large numbers in the days of Accius; there was a *Societas cantorum Graecorum* at Rome then: see *Raccolta in onore G. Lombroso*, 287. In England the early companies that played the interludes seldom numbered over four, and yet they had at times to take care of sixteen or more rôles. Doubling was less drastic in Shakespeare's theater but it sufficed to allow the dramatist the privilege of producing diversified effects by using many rôles for only one scene or act. In *Hamlet* alone there are some ten rôles of this type. Plautus and Terence do not hesitate to dismiss a character after the first scene or indeed to introduce one in the last.

influence upon Plautus which he had to bear constantly in mind. It kept many scenes rather thin. When, for instance, in the *Rudens* after the young man has been searching for his sweetheart through three acts, and after he has just learned that she has been rescued from a shipwreck and a thieving slave-dealer, he suddenly comes face to face with her at last, one naturally expects at least a cheerful exchange of greetings. But he has not a word for her. It takes us aback unless we notice that the girl must be represented on the stage by a mute, because the actor who has been playing her rôle must now be engaged in playing another part. Or again, in the *Pseudolus*, where Ballio heaps abuse upon three characters, sends them off, engages in a futile monologue, and then calls out three others and continues his tirade, one comprehends the strange interruption by noticing that the second trio cannot exist until the first three actors have gone in and changed their garbs and voices. It will be remembered that Shakespeare suffered from the same technical difficulty. At the end of the *Winter's Tale* we see far less of Perdita than we desire and we are hardly consoled by the knowledge that the actor who has been playing her rôle is now busy playing Hermione. Terence was not hampered to quite the same extent as Plautus by a lack of players, but the Greek convention reasserted itself later and was foolishly accepted in Horace's *Ars Poetica* to the detriment of the later drama.

As we have said, the early Roman dramatists did not use masks and in fact employed the most simple make-up in quickly adjusted garments and wigs. With the extensive doubling and trebling of rôles there must have been an uncomfortable amount of recognizing of the actors. The late scholiasts like Donatus, who discuss these matters, wrote when masks were again unusual but when actors were more plentiful. They are therefore somewhat obscure about the earlier custom. Their guess that Roscius introduced the mask[17] to hide an ineffectual countenance may be true, but it is very likely that the Greek masks were introduced on the Roman stage—this happened about the Gracchan time—in order to facilitate the doubling of rôles and to remove the confusion that arose from the easy recognition of the actors. By that time Rome was so large and the theater crowd so extensive that the play of features would at any rate be missed by a large part of the audience, and the well-marked masks served the useful purpose of distinguishing the characters at a distance. Opera glasses have now removed that necessity.

There seems to be some misunderstanding about the social status of the Roman actors because our sources of information are late and do not always distinguish between the various periods. The facts now available seem to warrant the statement that slaves were not employed as actors during the first hundred years of the drama when most of the great comedies were written and produced. At that time the authors usually acted themselves, and authors and actors were united in a common guild, honored by the state in the Alexandrian manner by being assigned an official meeting place at Minerva's

[17] Diomedes, in *G. L. K.*, I, 489, *quod oculis perversis erat*. The late commentators seem to have had very little information on the subject.

temple. Livius and Terence were freedmen, to be
sure, but out of respect for their art both were
highly honored by the foremost men of the senate.
The day when slaves had stigmatized the professions by their participation was still far off. Even
in Sulla's time the great rôles of legitimate comedy
and tragedy were assumed by distinguished men like
Roscius and Aesopus,[18] men whom Cicero was
pleased to number among his friends. Actors gradually lost their position in society only by the deterioration of the drama—of which we shall speak later.
It was apparently when the standard plays had to
give way to farces and mimes that slaves had to
be trained to take rôles which self-respecting citizens
refused to play. Then the social brand was marked
on the few who demeaned themselves by playing
with the slaves. And thus in the late Republic we
hear not a little of the cheapness of the actor's profession. However, that stigma did not even then
apply to the great actors who confined themselves
to the parts of the good old plays. The exact story
of the fall of the profession is lost to us. Cicero is
quoted as having said in his *De Republica* that at
Rome actors and others who took part in a profession of entertainment were deprived of their civic
rights and had their names struck off the tribal
registration list by the censors.[19] These words are

[18] On Roscius, see Von der Mühll *in* Pauly-Wiss. *sub. voc.*, 1123.
There is no evidence whatever for the traditional conjecture that
Roscius and Aesopus were freedmen. The sister of Roscius married
into a well-known family. Aesopus was probably a Greek who, like
Archias, had been given citizenship in some municipality as an honor.
His position at Rome was such that it is impossible to suppose that he
had ever been a slave.

[19] Cic., *De Rep.* iv 10; Livy VII, 2, is full of anachronisms. Cf. Warnecke, *Neue Jahrb.* 1914, 94. However, Warnecke fails to note how late
the evidence is and how completely it disagrees with the known circum-

assigned to Scipio in a dialogue whose dramatic date is 129 B.C. but, as in several other instances, Cicero may be allowing himself an anachronism. Livy happens to say, without specifying a date, that actors could not serve as soldiers in the Roman legions.

Now there are two possible explanations for this censorial stigma. It is possible that at one of the several puritanic assaults on the theater in the second century B.C.—and during one of these periods of reform the censor Nasica ordered a partly constructed theater to be torn down—a censorial brand may have been placed on the actors in order to discourage citizens from entering the profession. But it is quite as possible that in the early days when actors were difficult to secure for the public festivals some praetor in charge of the festival induced the censor to excuse actors from army service and that, following the Roman practice of using the military rôle for the voting list, he also struck the names of actors from the lists of the tribus. Later when the state was demoralized and slaves had filled the profession, the cancellation of the name, at first effected for practical purposes, may have been continued as morally appropriate. In Roscius' day the stigma was associated not with appearance on the stage but with playing for remuneration, so that when Roscius ceased to accept a fee he could be raised to the knighthood by Sulla. This fact proves

stances of the early Roman drama. Plautus, *Cist.* 785, which promises a flogging to the incapable actor, is of course one of the jokes of the play. The ninth article of the recently discovered charter of Cyrene excuses from certain public service various people (including doctors and teachers of music) who are engaged in professions of public welfare. Since the actors' guild at Rome was based upon Alexandrian models, it is not unlikely that certain Ptolemaic regulations were also taken over.

how unstable the theory of the actors' disability
really is and rather supports the view that removal
from the tribal list was not at first intended so much
as a stigma as an excuse from performing service
away from Rome. At any rate the social brand did
not apply to recognized actors in the standard
drama.

CHAPTER IV

TERENCE AND HIS SUCCESSORS

Plautus lived in the most productive period of
Roman comedy. He happens to mention only one
rival, the aged Naevius, but from later sources we
learn of Caecilius, Licinius, Trabea, Atilius, Titinius,
and others who apparently began to write before
the death of Plautus. That all of these actually
staged plays we may be sure, since manuscripts had
no chance of surviving unless they came into the
official archives by way of purchase for production.
So numerous were the old manuscripts in these
archives that Plautus, who could at most not have
written more than thirty or forty plays, was later
credited with a hundred and thirty. Apparently
unsigned plays were attributed to him because of
the commercial value of his name. But the fact
that so many stray plays were in existence is significant of the activity of writers. It is not surprising therefore that a guild of "writers and actors"
flourished in the days of Plautus, and that the state
recognized it and assigned it quarters on the Aventine.

Of the earlier men from whose works we have
fragments, only two are in any way individualized
in the scant remains. Titinius, who seems to have
been a late rival of Plautus, was so thoroughly lost
to his successors that Cicero seems not to have been
aware of him. But Varro refers to Titinius in high

terms in his work on the Latin language, written while he was gathering books for Caesar's projected public library. Varro probably was the man who ferreted out his plays and name from the aediles' archives. It is signal praise that Varro gives Titinius when he places him by the side of Terence as a delineator of character. An allusion to one of his plays by Horace seems to indicate that some of his work was actually staged in the early Empire (more than a hundred years after the dramatist's death) for the poet refers to a scene that is visualized rather than to a line read, and he assumes that Augustus will recognize his allusion.[1]

What Titinius did was to follow a suggestion made by Naevius and write original comedies (*togatae*) with native plots, scenes, and characters. When we recall how Plautus found it prudent to cling to Greek plots for social and moral reasons, we see that Titinius must have had a vein of daring. That he was lauded among the very foremost for characterization is the more remarkable since he did not adapt characters already well outlined. It was no easy task to present before the old Catonian society comedies revolving about Roman men and women, and to rival the plays of Plautus which could legitimately appropriate all the attractive plots of Hellenistic Athens. Donatus remarks naïvely that realistic Roman comedy of the old day, unlike the Greek comedy, could not picture slaves as more clever than their masters. This statement, of course, does not go to the heart of the matter, but it is one way of saying that the Romans, who in-

[1] Horace, *Epist.* I, 13: he mentions Pyrrha's posture on the stage.

sisted on social decorum in home life, were in no mood
to see themselves pictured as the gulls of spoiled
sons and saucy slaves. If the togata had to eliminate all such scenes, it must have altered the whole
tone of comedy. But that was not all. We have
noticed how Plautus was compelled to change and
attenuate feminine rôles because the Romans had
nothing to put in the place of the semi-respectable
Greek hetaerae with whom the youth of Athens
associated freely. What was there for Titinius to
do in writing Roman plays? It was out of the question to insult the dignity of the noble household
with stories of boisterous love affairs; and yet he
apparently did not wish to sacrifice such plots either
by avoiding the female characters or by using those
that Roman society disdained. He did want the
love story and he wanted it both wholesome enough
to attract Rome and natural enough to give a free
play of emotions in an active plot, and he found it
in a way that Plautus had not. He abandoned the
jeunesse dorée of the standard Greek play and resorted to the natural and free society of the Italian
village communities outside of the great capital,
where, as in Italian villages of today, honest young
men and women of humble circumstances worked
together at daily tasks in shops, at counters, desks,
and work benches. Titinius made a real discovery
when he left the artificial society of aristocratic
Rome because it gave no opportunity for treating
of natural relations between the unmarried young
of both sexes and went out into the near-by villages
of Latium or the humbler streets of the city where
more normal conditions obtained. He was perhaps

the first writer of Roman comedy who could draw his material from life and still base his comedy on a love story. Only fifteen titles of his plays have survived, but nine of these take their name from the leading female characters in the plays: *The Maid of Setia, The Lady of the Dye Shop, The Girl of Velitrae, The Twin Sister, the Girl Who Knows Something about the Law, The Stepmother, Pyrrha the Weaver, The Dancing Girl of Ferentinum, The Flute-player* and *The Girl of Ulubrae.* These heroines are folk in humble life but the fragments show that they are none the less sprightly, quick-witted and interesting creatures. Today we are sadly at a loss in trying to comprehend the life of the great masses of the people during the Plautine period. Plautus in his re-shapings of Greek plots reflects it only in his suppressions and intimations, and then very imperfectly. Livy in his dignified and voluminous history of this period strides majestically over it. We would gladly surrender much of both for the faithful and sympathetic picture that a volume of Titinius could give us. If Varro's judgment was right in lauding the power of characterization of this author we might, if he were rescued, find him a place by the side of very modern realists.

Caecilius Statius is the other writer of comedy vying with Plautus of whom something is known, and he too deserves to be remembered with a keen hope that his works may some day come to light. He was more orthodox than Titinius, kept, like Plautus, more or less close to his Greek models, and obeyed the same social purpose of not offending puritanic taste by dressing his players in Greek garb.

Strange to say, he was a Celt, the first in the history
of literature. He had apparently been captured as
a boy somewhere near Milan when the Romans
were campaigning there during the Hannibalic war.
That he was not a mere child at the time becomes
evident from the fact that he never wrote Latin
quite well enough to suit the discriminating ear of
Cicero—who otherwise read him with pleasure. Yet
he somehow received a good education—as bright
slaves often did—for he knew Greek well. He also
got his freedom somehow and became a close associate of Ennius. He lived long enough to give aid
to Terence in the production of that young man's
first youthful play, the *Andria*, and was generous
enough to recommend the play to the aediles when
they hesitated to accept it. Ambivius, the loyal
producer of Terence, remarks in one of the prologues which he spoke for Terence that Caecilius
had had a discouraging series of rejections in his
youth but that he, Ambivius, confident of the poet's
worth, had persisted in presenting the plays till success was assured.[2] A later critic, Volcacius—who,
to be sure, takes no account of the togatae in this
particular list—places Caecilius at the very head of
the writers of comedy, giving Plautus second place
and Terence sixth. Unfortunately we do not happen
to know whether this critic was a man of sound
judgment.

The plays of Caecilius were constructed much
like those of Plautus, with the same dependence
upon the Greeks in plot, and with the same devotion
to Roman musical accompaniment and to arial mon-

[2] Terence, *Hecyra*, 15–20.

odies. His use of the splendidly rhythmical trochaic septenarii is everywhere noticeable in the fragments. Varro suggests that Caecilius was esteemed rather for his melodramatic effects than for his ability to create characters, in this matter regarding him less highly than Terence, and praises him especially for the composition of his plots. Just why Varro admired his plots he did not say, but if, as we may suspect, Caecilius was the first dramatist to abandon the Greek and early Roman manner of disclosing the trend of the plot in prologues and to focus the interest of his comedies more upon suspense and surprise, Varro's judgment would be justified. We make this suggestion because, as we shall explain, Terence's methods were unconventional in this respect, and Terence in writing his comedies had had the advice of Caecilius. If Caecilius was an innovator in this matter, it would account not only for Varro's high opinion of his plots but also for the fact that Caecilius failed at first to attract an audience used to explicit preparation. In the end, however, Caecilius succeeded and it would seem that he wore well. Manuscripts of his plays apparently were dug out of the archives early for re-staging, and revivals were frequent. Cicero knew his works well enough to quote from several of them even when far from his library. Horace alludes to a character of his in the *Ars Poetica*, and in the second-century craze for the early Latin authors Caecilius kept his place among the foremost.

The six plays of Terence are so well known that little need be said by way of general characterization. It is generally supposed that they are more faithful paraphrases of Greek originals than any of the Plautine comedies. This idea, based partly upon the fact that Terence used the older Greek dramatic form instead of adopting the Plautine custom of introducing cantica, and partly upon the fact that Donatus' commentary mentions relatively few departures from the Greek, is probably correct. There is also good reason for supposing that Terence might care to reproduce his Greek model with more fidelity than Plautus could. Society had changed so much between 200 and 160 B.C. that the Greek plays could be presented without alteration, even to the point of placing on the stage attractive hetaerae. Moreover, education was general enough so that cultivated persons desired more finished plays and an elimination of some of the Plautine downrightness. The plays of Terence though less amusing than those of Plautus are on a higher literary plane and much of their beauty undoubtedly savors of the delicate humanity that may be found in the recently discovered plays of Menander. Nevertheless we must wait till the actual models of Terence's comedies are discovered before we deny these graces to Terence himself. We happen to know from Donatus that three of the characters of the *Andria* were introduced by Terence into his paraphrase of a Menandrian plot. While the rôles are somewhat stilted the characters give expression to some of those penetrating observations that critics are wont to attribute to the original.[3] This proves that Terence

[3] See Wessner, *Aemilius Asper.* E.g., the refusal of Charinus to win his love by unworthy threats (317), and Pamphilus' refusal to take credit for a deed which he says a gentleman could not fail to perform (330). It should also be noticed that in the *Perinthia* Menander had a scene of brutal slave-torturing which Terence took the liberty of eliminating.

was himself capable of very delicate feeling, and until we find his originals it is therefore scientifically defensible to acknowledge Terence as the possible source of some of the best passages in these six comedies.

It has frequently been noticed[4] that the writers of the New Comedy, including Plautus, were far more generous than present-day dramatists in "preparing" their audiences for every turn in the plot and that they depended less for their effects upon the elements of "suspense" and "surprise." It is generally assumed that the expository prologue was adopted by comedy from tragedy in order that the unlettered spectators who crowded the theater at the festivals should not have any difficulty in following the play. It has also been noted repeatedly that when the interest of the play did not rest in comic situations, buffoonery, ludicrous characters, and the like, but rather in an intricate plot that was solved at the end by a "recognition" or some other unforeseen event, it was necessary to introduce an omniscient "prologue" to explain the situation in an expository monologue. Superhumans like Heros, Agnoia, Elenchus, Tyche, Aer, Auxilium, Arcturus, Fides, and Lar were used, or an abstract "prologus" who could be conceived of as knowing not only the complete situation but also the outcome of the play. Only when the plot was so simple that it unfolded without risk of misconception, could the exposition be trusted to characters or expository dialogue within the play.

[4] Cf. especially Leo, *Plaut. Forsch.* chap. IV; Legrand, *Daos*, 490 ff.; Michaut, *Plaute*, II, 116 ff.; Wilamowitz, *Menander, Das Schiedsgericht*, 142 ff. A part of this chapter has appeared in the *Am. Jour. Phil.*, 1928, 309.

Such observations may be accepted as correct so far as they go. However, they do not sufficiently explain the controlling purpose of over-explicit preparation, the consequences of it in dramatic effect, and a noticeable endeavor in Terence's day to break loose from the limitations of the device. It is doubtful, for example, whether suspense and surprise were avoided merely because of certain intellectual limitations on the part of Menander's spectators; indeed it is probable that explicit "preparation" was a convention that held the boards without serious objection till Terence experimented in a new method.

Greek New Comedy was shaped in the fourth century for audiences accustomed to the dramatic technique developed upon the tragic stage. Antiphanes reveals clearly in a well-known passage what the audience expected (Kock, II, *Antiphanes* 191): "Fortunate the task of the tragic poet! Before a word is spoken, the spectator knows the theme . . . . at the mere mention of the name Oedipus he knows the rest." Then he proceeds to say that the writer of comedy had to prepare the audience in every detail, since if a single item was missed the spectator started to hiss. This reveals the fact that in viewing a comedy the spectator expected not only to know the situation but also to have a clear clue to the solution, just as he had when viewing tragedies. The well-known prologues of Euripides did not have to foretell as well as prepare; a prologue in tragedy needed at most to remind the spectators of the main outline of the tale and to show the point at which action started. Euripides was well aware that most of his audience would at once know what the end of the story would be.[5] Now if the outcome was foreseen, the ancient dramatist, unlike the modern, could obviously not make free use of suspense and surprise. The writer of tragedy had to draw his emotional values from the pity of a well-informed audience viewing "with a sense of fear or dread" the groping of characters involved in the meshes of fate. Thus the obvious consequence of the use of a known plot was of course dependence upon the theme of *fate*, the constant employment of gloomy foreshadowing, the use with frequent reiteration of what has been called "tragic irony." There seems to be a feeling in Aristotle that "pity and dread" are the essential elements of tragedy, but it is safe to say that had Greek tragedy frequently used invented plots Aristotle would have found that sympathetic suspense with catastrophic surprise would rather have been employed to produce the tragic catharsis, and would have been equally effective.

In studying the new comedy we may assume with Antiphanes, and on the basis of Menander, that the writer thought out his plot in terms of this well-established technique. In that case an omniscient prologue must give the situation and give it more explicitly than in tragedy because he had to do much more than remind. He must present the whole situation and in addition he must give explicit hints of the solution, if the spectator was to have the same advantage as he had in tragedy

---

[5] One may add that if he was more explicit than one would think necessary he was perhaps giving aid to the many strangers that came to the theater in his day.

where the solution was a matter of common knowledge. That is the new element forced upon the writer of comedy by fifth-century convention. In Menander's *Perikeiromene*, for example, the deferred prologue, Agnoia, not only gives the situation but adds: "this was done . . . . in order to start the train of revelations, so that in time these people might discover their kin."

So in Plautus, wherever we have an intricate play that develops to a conclusion which could not be revealed by the characters, the prologue, if it has survived, discloses the outcome to the audience. In the *Poenulus* the prologus anticipates the solution when he says (line 245) that the father will come and find his daughter. In the *Rudens* the North Star not only has seen all that has occurred before the opening scene but he reveals the secret of the last act by saying that the girl is the old man's daughter, and that the lover will appear presently (33 ff. and 80). In the *Amphitruo*, Mercury, one of the actors, can serve as prologue because he is omniscient. He tells the spectators how to distinguish the characters and says (140–48) that *Amphitruo* is about to come. The rest was known to the audience because this play, like the tragedies, was based upon a myth. In the *Aulularia*, the Spirit of the Hearth narrates what it is necessary to know of the past and then adds, "I shall make our neighbor propose marriage to the girl so as to compel the young man to do so" (31 ff.). In the *Captives* the prologue informs us that Tyndarus is Hegio's unrecognized son who will come into his own presently and that the other son will also be found. The prologue of the *Casina* concludes the exposition by the revelation that the girl will turn out to be a freeborn citizen.

And this regard for the fullest preparation of the audience goes far beyond the prologue and the expository first act. Most of the intrigues devised to further the action are first explained, or at least discussed or suggested before they are actually carried out. Any student of Plautus will think of scores of examples: of how Mercury tells the spectators that he is going to climb to the roof to mock at Amphitruo (997), how in the *Miles* the plan to rescue the girl is explained before it is carried out, how in the *Poenulus* (550) the trick by which the slave-dealer is to be imposed upon is worked out on the stage before it is played,[6] etc.

Now of course this sort of exposition is too explicit to satisfy modern taste.[7] It is sometimes excused with the reminder that ancient comedies were written for a single performance and must be understood at first presentation without the aid of reviewers' comments or playbills; and it is sometimes explained as a concession to witless audiences—on whom Horace, following Peripatetic critics, blamed most literary crudities. Such explanations sufficed in the days when we could attribute this undue explicitness to Plautus, but now that we have

[6] For other instances see *Miles*, 238, 381, 767, 904, 1170; *Pseud.*, 725; *Casina*, 683; *Most.*, 662; *Menaechmi*, 831; *Trin.* 1137; cf. Legrand, *Daos*, 533 ff.

[7] The *Merry Wives of Windsor*, though it contains no prologue, is fully as explicit in the preparation of every incident—even the two basket-scenes—as any play of Plautus. Indeed most of Shakespeare's plays give more attention to preparation than is customary on the stage today even though his plots were usually familiar ones. The *Romeo and Juliet* even has a prologue which goes so far as to disclose the outcome.

discovered Menander given to the same type of technique we ought to look farther. The important fact seems to be that the Greek audience was accustomed to preparation and to the devices which the consequent construction of the play demanded, and that the originators of the early New Comedy followed custom. And since in tragedy the general knowledge of the myths used in the plots obviated use of unexpected catastrophes and compelled writers to find compensation in tragic irony, so the adoption of the same method of plot construction for comedy eliminated the use of tension and increased the employment of a kind of comic irony. The effects of this comic irony range all the way from what Aristotle terms educated insolence (πεπαιδευμένη ὕβρις) to genial and sympathetic fellow-feeling, according as the victim of the delusion is a villain, a braggart, a buffoon, or a harmless innocent. The foreknowledge which the audience has of what the players are unconsciously stumbling into provides both the "sense of superiority," which Plato found to be an effect of comedy, and the enjoyment of the incongruous which moderns have often considered its chief ingredient. This comic irony, concocted like its counterpart in tragedy, is a large part of the stock in trade of Menander and of Plautus.

In the *Captives* of Plautus the audience knows that Hegio has his own son before him in chains, and notices that, not recognizing his son, he causes him much suffering. Throughout the play the attentive spectator will watch for the very effective incongruities that arise from the father's ignorance.

In the *Rudens*, Daemones, not knowing that the
girl who is trying to escape from shipwreck and the
slave-dealer is his own daughter, at first seems to
the informed spectator extremely insensitive to her
suffering. The father's sympathies are aroused only
indirectly by his religious respect for a suppliant at
the altar, then by the accident of being called in to
arbitrate regarding her basket of birth tokens. Only
when he has established her civil status by this accidental judgment does he learn the truth. In a more
farcical form comic irony is freely used in the plays
of self-deception, for example in the case of a brag-
ging coward like the *Miles Gloriosus*, or in plays
depending upon mistaken identity or some similar
delusion, as in the *Menaechmi* and the *Amphitruo*.
And in very nearly all the plays of Plautus, if it
be not the chief mainstay of the plot, it appears
at least here and there.

The new fragments of Menander prove that
Menander had frequently constructed his plays with
this effect in mind. Indeed it is the decisive factor
in all that are extensive enough to permit of analysis.
In the *Arbitrants* Smicrines all unconsciously arbi-
trates against his own child. In the *Samia* the old
man is misled by a chance remark into the belief
that his son has betrayed him, and the resulting
irony runs through the central part of the play.
And even when the facts are disclosed the son immediately sets going another series of misunderstand-
ings (disclosed beforehand to the audience, line 432)
by threatening to go into exile. The *Perikeiromene*
is built about the same device. Two men are in
love with the same maiden. One is her unrecog-

nized brother, the other is jealous of her attentions to the former. The girl knows that the former is her brother but may not reveal the fact. However, the deity, Agnoia, has informed the spectators of the relationship so that they are in a position to view the intricate play at cross-purposes, but there is little of what we should call suspense because they have also been informed that a recognition scene will end the play satisfactorily.

In the *Hero* the expository prologue is lost, but we know that the prologue was the omniscient *Heros*, who adequately prepared the audience for what was to follow.[8] Here a husband (unrecognized), his wife, their "exposed daughter," not yet known as such, and two lovers of this daughter, one a slave, the other a rich neighbor, all enter a tangle of delusion to which the audience has the key. In the *Georgos* a man expresses to a woman his desire to marry her daughter. He does not know that he is the girl's father. As the woman—bound to secrecy—stands wringing her hands in despair, the audience—apparently informed of the secret—experiences a situation as poignant as that of the *Oedipus*. And finally in the Petrograd fragment of the *Phasma* we find a mother's furtive visits to her daughter, born out of wedlock, and an entangled love affair, a situation which again involves the use of irony, since a fragment from the prologue shows us that the audience has been informed in advance.

It would be hazardous to say that Menander always lets the spectator into the secret beforehand

[8] The expository dialogue between the two slaves gives the immediate situation so plainly that a *Heros* would hardly have been employed for the prologue except to reveal the secret hidden to the characters.

so as to make use of dramatic irony, but it is striking that he does so in every instance where we possess enough of his plot in the original to test his methods. It is apparently his usual method of procedure. This is also in accord with his well-known predilection for Tyche, the counterpart in comedy of tragic fate. We need not suppose, as has often been done, that his constant reference to Tyche springs from his own philosophical doctrine. Such well-known passages as "Chance holds the helm; mortal forethought is but a delusion" (*Frag.*, Kock, 482), etc., are, of course, comments of characters in the play. They need not be expressions of the dramatist's own creed. But such comments would naturally come frequently in plays built on the conventional tragic form which required that the players grope their obscure way through the action in front of an audience which knew the end.

Now these observations are not meant as an attempt to rehabilitate Leo's doctrine that the New Comedy merely borrowed all its devices of prologue, fate, recognition, and the rest from tragedy. Prescott's incisive criticism[9] of that view must stand, with its insistence that we take Sicilian antecedents, Aristophanes, and environment into account. The new comedy was hardly as helplessly unoriginal as Leo held. The problem we have raised should rather be approached from the viewpoint of what the spectator expected and desired. It did not necessarily arise in the construction of plotless farces, in the presentation of ludicrous situations, buffoonery, and scenes centering about com-

[9] In *Class. Phil.* 1916, 125 ff.; 1917, 405 ff.; 1918, 113 ff.; 1919, 108 ff.

ical and preposterous characters. When, however, the plot was involved and a long consistent story was to be unraveled, the spectators, who knew nothing of the story, desired to be put at the same point of vantage early in the play that they naturally enjoyed when an *Oedipus*, a *Medea*, or an *Orestes* was presented.

When we turn to the Roman stage we seem to discover an attempt to break away from this convention, if not in Plautus[10] at least in Terence. We do not find conclusive evidence that Plautus seriously changed the construction of the Greek plots which he used except to remove the choral interludes and turn the plays into musical comedies, though it is likely that he usually avoided plays that had very intricate plots, and chose freely from those that contained laughter-producing situations. There is no evidence that he sought for suspense, or revamped any of his originals in order to attain it.

Terence, however, despite his fondness for the Greek originals and his outspoken claim of fidelity to them, seems consciously to have striven for a suspended dénouement. He does not entirely suppress dramatic irony, but he reduces its scope, he eliminates the expository prologue completely, he is chary about giving information to the spectator, preferring to keep him under tension for a part if not for the whole of the play.

A brief reference to the *Adelphoe*, his last play, will best reveal his procedure. Here two brothers

[10] The *Epidicus* probably once had a prologue (Wheeler, *Am. Jour. Phil.* 1917, 264). One may suspect that the play in its present form—which requires as patient reading as the *Hecyra*—was due to a post-Terentian revision. The *Mercator* has a prologue that does not reveal much of the plot but in the second act the outcome is hinted at by way of a dream. The play as we have it is a revision.

employ different methods in bringing up their sons. Micio, who has adopted one of Demea's sons, is indulgent, Demea is severe. Both boys enjoy themselves, Micio's confessedly, Demea's secretly. In fact the latter throws the burden of his escapades on Micio's son. Hence when the action begins (1. 182) Demea is found scolding Micio because Micio's son is setting a bad example to his supposedly virtuous brother. This is completely in Menander's ironic style, for, as we shall see, Menander in the original had a prologue informing the audience that Demea's son was the rascal of the two boys.

In Terence's version, however, there is no expository prologue; the audience does not yet know the secret that Demea's son is the source of the mischief. The irony is not wholly lost to those who have a good enough memory to recall half an hour later how misplaced Demea's rebukes actually were. Terence is accumulating effects by suspending the revelation which Menander gave at once. But he goes even further in increasing tension. The prologue of the original had explained the bold deed that started the action, namely, that Micio's son, in order to aid his brother, had forcibly taken from the slave-dealer the girl whom his brother loved but had not the money to buy or the courage to steal. That fact had to be presented somehow, so Terence, according to Donatus, inserts a scene in Act II which conveys the desired impression. Characteristically Terence still withholds the crucial fact that the boy is committing this crime not for himself but for his brother. Perhaps the shrewder spectators would suspect the truth. In Menander's play they knew it from the first and laughed at Demea's misplaced boasts. In Terence's adaptation, however, they continue in doubt. It is not till a fourth of the play is over that Terence solves this mystery. He holds it back so long indeed that there is danger that the spectator may go too far on a mistaken clue. After the revelation, however, the audience, acquainted with a situation that Demea still fails to comprehend, can proceed for several scenes to enjoy the dramatic irony involved in this circumstance.

But Terence has one more surprise in store at the very end, to which Donatus again supplies the clue for us. At the end of the play Menander had suggested a partial conversion of Demea, while Micio went smiling to the final scene. Not so Terence. Writing for a more puritanic Roman audience, he felt the need of giving an appreciable rebuke to Micio for his lack of principle, and hence compelled him by way of consistency in his easy generosity to marry an unattractive widow.[11] In other words, with a minimum of changes in his paraphrase, Terence, without greatly reducing the dramatic irony inherent in the separate scenes, has so adapted a standard Menandrian plot based upon self-delusion (for which the spectator is prepared) that the elements of suspense and surprise have become vital factors. This seems to me to be Terence's favorite procedure.

[11] According to Donatus, Menander's play also contained the marriage, but without objection on the part of Micio. Since in Terence Micio is represented as resisting, the marriage must have been considered as punishment.

In the *Andria*, which was Terence's first play, he apparently reveals the first hesitating attempt at this mode of constructing comedies. He tells us in the preface that he used Menander's *Andria* in the main with suggestions from the *Perinthia*, and the Menandrian fragments of these two plays which can be identified in Terence are fairly well scattered through the *Andria*. Donatus states that the rôles of Charinus, Byrrhia, and Sosia were added by Terence. Charinus and Byrrhia are so involved in the action of five central scenes that Terence must have re-shaped the play very much in order to include these characters. Since in a recognition scene near the end the heroine turns out to be a citizen we now have a right to assume that Menander's *Andria* probably had a prologue revealing this fact. Terence omits the prologue and, therefore, the usual key. But he does not dare, as in the *Hecyra*, his next play, to rely upon his audience's being patient until the recognition scene. In the middle of the second act (line 221) he drops the rather broad hint in a monologue: "they have set the story going that the girl is an Athenian." That would be enough to prevent the spectators from following false leads. The *Andria*, therefore, seems to reveal Terence's first attempt at constructing a play in which a deferred hint took the place of full preparation. One wonders whether the aged Caecilius, who helped Terence with this play, may have used the device before Terence and suggested it to him.

In the *Hecyra*, the second play of Terence, there is no preparation, and the delay in relieving the tension of the spectator is carried to extreme lengths. The old story of a maiden violated at the festival during a dark night provides the entanglement. In the end the guilty father of her child turns out to be the very man she has married. Even through the Latin text one can see that the early scenes of the original[12] presupposed an informed audience enjoying the delusions of characters working on mistaken suppositions. But Terence blotted out the information by deleting the prologue of the original. The semi-expository first act gives the immediate situation but reserves the key-fact for line 829 near the end of the play. If that fact—that the unknown violator was Pamphilus, the husband—had been revealed to the spectators at the beginning they might have enjoyed the dramatic irony of the scene (II, 1) in which Laches scolds his wife for imagined wrongs, and especially the incongruity of Pamphilus' oath, by all that is sacred, that he is not to blame for the separation (line 476). Terence has done a very daring thing here in keeping the audience in doubt and in anxiety. He has assumed that the audience will patiently bear in mind these puzzling quarrels and asseverations and watch the mysteries accumulating without any key to the solution for

[12] The *Hecyra* according to Donatus was modeled upon a play of Apollodorus, but it is now clear that that play was in turn modeled upon Menander's *Arbitrants*. That Terence suppressed the prologue of Apollodorus is apparent from the comment of Donatus (who had a copy of the Greek play at hand) on 1.58: *Hoc* (the use of *protatica prosopa*) *maluit Terentius quam per prologum narraret argumentum aut* θεὸν ἀπὸ μηχανῆς *induceret loqui*. Since the list of characters and the beginning of Menander's *Arbitrants* are lost, there may be some doubt regarding his use of preparation in this play, but since the whole play operates with "dramatic irony" and since Apollodorus had a prologue, it is more than likely that he "prepared" his audience here as elsewhere. At any rate Menander's audience discover the owner of the finger ring in the second act.

several hundred lines. A modern, used to that kind of thing in detective stories, finds it less difficult to do, but our students usually have to read the *Hecyra* with unusually alert attention, and it is certain that they would miss much of the delicate play if they were to see it hurriedly acted on the stage without previous preparation. In fact, Terence commits the sin of hinting at incorrect solutions. Pamphilus (at line 260) learns of the child and only betrays bewilderment, which is apt to mislead the spectator; at line 517 Pamphilus' father also learns of the child but draws an incorrent conclusion, giving a new starting point for a possible erroneous guess; at line 577 his mother, half-informed, imagines that her son has deserted his wife for ugly reasons. Only at line 827 does the resolution of the intrigue take place. There is not one ancient play before the day of Terence, so far as we know, where an audience was left in such complete suspense before an accumulating mass of perplexities; and this was an audience, it will be remembered, accustomed to be taken into the confidence of the prologue. It is not surprising, therefore, that this play—one of the most human in the classical repertoire—failed twice, and that the spectators rushed away from it to see a boxing match. But Terence apparently was proud of what he had done and insisted that the play have its chance. Only after he had established his reputation by the success of the *Eunuchus* was it at last played with success.

The *Heautontimoroumenos*, produced two years after the failure of the *Hecyra*, puts less strain upon the audience, since half the secret—that Clinea's sweetheart has proved faithful and worthy of him—is disclosed fairly early (line 243). From that point the spectators are permitted without too much anxiety to enjoy the dramatic irony involved in the delusions of the over-confident Chremes who bestows on his neighbor the pity that is his own due. Soon after the middle of the play (675 ff.) the spectators are admitted to the last important fact, namely, that Clinea's sweetheart is freeborn, while the impossible courtesan seems likely to become Chremes' daughter-in-law. Since, however, Chremes refuses to accept the evidence of his own eyes, the self-delusion only increases the irony, and the play continues from that point in the Menandrian style. The play is indeed one of the best in point of construction, since by abandoning the expository prologue[13] Terence was enabled to accumulate mysteries which he gradually solved in such a way as to substitute Menandrian satire for tension.

In the *Eunuchus* Terence for once shifts to the Plautine manner, resting his play chiefly on buffoons, imposture, and ludicrous situations. Indeed he borrows caricatures from another play in order to cram in the fun. There is no prologue, but none was needed. Thais stands self-revealed from the first scene, while Pamphila's station is more than hinted at in the second scene. The tricking of a braggart captain did not involve much anxiety, even though the preparation is slight. The play is full of fun and easy to follow. Terence had for

[13] I assume that Menander had revealed something about the escapades of Chremes' own son in the prologue, since Chremes' pretenses at knowing how to bring up children (152 ff.) were doubtless written in the first place to amuse an audience that foresaw his failure.

once yielded to popular demand and he was materially rewarded. It was the only play of his that was immediately put on a second time, and the aediles paid for it what was then considered the very high sum of 8000 sesterces.

The *Phormio*, like the *Heauton* and the *Adelphoe*, employs a good mingling of suspense and preparation. There is no expository prologue. That one existed in the original is probable from the occurrence of such unconscious allusions to actuality as the story concocted in court that the girl was a kinswoman (line 117). The fact that Chremes has a daughter like the one in question is not made known to the audience till half the play is over—a restraint which is surpassed only in the *Hecyra*. However, from line 570 the solution is surmised and it finally is evident at line 755. Henceforth the interest is provided by a series of quick though unprepared-for surprises.

Whether or not Terence should have all the credit for breaking away from the old conventional construction imposed on tragedy by the accident that the plots were known, we cannot say. It is not likely that Menander introduced this innovation, since all the plots that have recently been discovered seem to retain the older construction. Plautus, except in plays subsequently revised, like the *Epidicus* and the *Mercator*, is true to the convention every time that his plot is intricate and ends with an important "discovery." We have suggested that Caecilius, who was Terence's critic in his first play, may possibly have shown the way since he somehow gained fame for his plot construction. But we have no definite evidence of this. At any rate the modernization comes after Plautus and seems, therefore, to be a discovery of the Roman stage. It might be claimed that the discovery was due to the accident that the prologue was desired for the expression of the author's personal opinion, so that it was not available for exposition.[14] However, this would not explain Terence's procedure. In the *Adelphoe*, for instance, he seems to transfer some of the exposition from the eliminated prologue to the opening monologue of Micio. What is noticeable is that he here gives a very chary exposition in the monologue, gives some more details in the inserted kidnaping scene, and yet carefully withholds the secret—which could so easily have been disclosed—that the girl was stolen for the supposedly virtuous brother. In a word, Terence is conscious of what he is doing. He has apparently eliminated the expository prologue purposely in order to rid himself of an old convention and to intensify comedy by injecting into his plots the elements of surprise and suspense.

After Terence the aediles seem to have saved money by resorting freely to the archives and reviving old plays. At any rate many of the Plautine comedies bear signs of having been tampered with at this time. Long speeches were cut, explicit prologues were excised or reduced so as to introduce

---

[14] Leo, *Gesch. Lit.*, 218, assumes that Caecilius had used the prologue for personal criticism; Euanthius III. 2 says *deos argumentis narrandis machinatos ceteri Latini ad instar Graecorum habent, Terentius non habet*, which of course does not exclude an occasional use of the personal prologue. After Terence, Afranius sometimes employs superhuman prologues (Priapus, Sapientia, and Remeligo), but he seems also to have used the prologue for personal statements in the manner of Terence (lines 25–8).

the element of surprise. In other words, the comedies were modernized in type and given speed. It is more than likely that this refurbishing of old plays discouraged young writers, since the generation following Terence left few names of dramatists to posterity. Only Turpilius, who worked in the Plautine tradition, was well known later. He died at a very old age about 103 B.C.

The togata, however, kept its place better through the voluminous contributions of Afranius, whose *floruit* was just before the Gracchan day. Of his works, praised by such fair judges as Cicero, Horace, and Quintilian, we have some seventy titles and over six hundred lines. By mere chance, we hear of a revival of a play of his in Caesar's day and of another even in Nero's time. Rome was now cosmopolitan enough so that a writer of comedy need not limit his range. In matter and sentiment Afranius reminded critics of Menander and Terence, yet his fragments show that, like Plautus, he availed himself of the advantages of very generous musical accompaniments. The most striking reference to him which has come down to us is that of Seneca who says that Afranius blended the spirit of comedy and tragedy in his work. If we may judge from this statement he may in this respect have been a precursor of Molière. After Afranius came Atta who has left us a dozen bare titles and little else.

But legitimate comedy was doomed at Rome. On festival days the populace had to be amused, and the Roman populace was rapidly changing in character as slavery was pushing out free labor. Even before the Gracchan reform Scipio the younger could face the crowds of the Forum with the remark that most of them had come to Rome as slaves. The Gracchans did not improve the quality of those crowds when they instituted the corn-doles. The free manumission of slaves was creating a polyglot proletariat which corn doles now tended to keep in the city, where they were fed and amused. In response to the desires of such folk, chariot races were made more exciting and the gladiatorial shows, introduced from Campania, became more frequent and more gruesome. Needless to say the well constructed plots of Plautus and Terence could not hold such audiences in their seats. The aediles and praetors, who wished to keep the entertainment on as high a level as possible, still persisted in producing some respectable plays at every festival, but to save their popularity in view of future elections they were driven to admit an increasing number of the more trivial plays as well.

After Sulla's time, though great actors like Roscius still played old rôles, the farce gained ground over the legitimate comedy. The farce, a more or less extemporaneous form, like the *commedia d'arte* shaped as much by the actors as by the authors, had long been in use as a brief epilogue to performances of tragedies. The form most frequently used was the so-called *Atellana*, named from an Oscan village in Campania which was captured by Rome during the Hannibalic war. At first Oscan players had presented these farces in the Oscan dialect. It is very likely that the many Campanians who were trying to make a living at Rome after they had been driven off their lands in 210 brought these amusing plays along to produce in the Oscan "colony" of Rome, and that in time the Romans discovered how entertaining they were and began to employ the players at festivals. One is reminded of how the producers of Vienna and Innsbruck have frequently invited the village players from the Tyrolese hill-towns to give their simple homemade comedies before sophisticated urban audiences.

The Atellan farces were usually spontaneous bits of improvised fun in which the witty players, unhampered by a fixed text, developed their own parts. There was much sameness of plot and rôle, usually a ridiculous situation at the expense of some extravagant character, the fat fellow, the old simpleton, the self-deluded wiseacre, the country bumpkin, or what not. There was also much display of countryside wisdom and frequently of broad and coarse wit. By Sulla's day various city-wits—we know the names of some and have more than a hundred titles of their works—exploited this old form and wrote Latin farces on the Atellan models, obeying literary conventions so far as to employ verse instead of prose. Even Sulla, who was a devotee of the theater, tried his hand at writing this style of comedy.

But these plays also had to give way to something lighter, namely the mime. Simple realistic mimes had appeared at unofficial folk festivals for many years before literature became aware of them. They avoided such artificiality as mask and extravagant garb. They alone employed actresses for female rôles. They got their names from their special devotion to mimicry and caricature, but they proceeded to invade the whole field of comedy; and had the respectable togata not been bound by convention to exclude actresses on the stage and to adopt the mask, there is no reason why the two should not have merged. In fact the mime came to be a more realistic togata, and as such might have played a dignified rôle in literature. And in Cicero's day there were writers like Laberius and actresses like Arbuscula and Cytheris who revealed an ambition to elevate the mime into the region of serious art. The fate of the mime, however, lay at the mercy of the rabble who demanded ever cheaper amusement. And the scenario writers of the late Republic and early Empire supplied it. They wrote plots and created female rôles that not even Arbuscula would play, and that self-respecting Romans would not go to see. And so the mime—which indeed lived on for centuries—fell into the class of the tawdriest performances.

The farces and the mimes, while incapable of embodying careful characterization or lines of any real literary value, could at their best provide a vehicle for current ideas and a fruitful entertainment in skilful caricature and much rollicking fun. Their descent to the lower strata of amusement was not so much the fault of the forms as of the audiences that determined their content. It is not surprising, therefore, that these audiences—eager for entertainment which might exclude all possibility of having to exercise the intellect—finally demanded an extravaganza that appealed solely to eye and ear.

Horace lived to see and bemoan the discovery of the pantomime which, as its name implies, was wholly mimicry, with nothing to disturb a lazy brain. What Pylades did with tragedy, Bathyllus of Alexandria did with comedy. He silently acted his rôles using interpretative gestures to the accompanying rhythms of seductive music. There at last the rabble found supreme satisfaction. But Horace at any rate in reviewing the history of the stage did not argue that every new change had marked progress. In his opinion the stage had descended to the lowest depth of inanity.

At Rome, as elsewhere, the drama had proved to be a fairly accurate barometer not of the culture of the educated classes but of the populace. Nothing in the form of official censorship had at any time exercised any serious effect upon the theater. The praetors and aediles were not to blame for what happened. They had placed good plays on the stage as long as could be expected at the risk of offending the masses. Time and again, relying upon their convictions as to the worth of a comedy, they had staged plays that had failed; they were willing to pay very high salaries, partly out of their own purses, to great actors like Aesopus and Roscius who tried to revive the best plays and to win back to the theater an intelligent group of listeners; they had set aside reserved seats first for the senators and later for the knights in order to secure good audiences for literary productions of a high order. Nevertheless the drama declined. What the people demanded had in the end to be provided.

Individual criticism probably served its purpose to some extent, but could not prevent the ebb. Men like Cicero ridiculed the cheap entertainments and refused to attend them, they went out of their way to encourage the better plays, and they did everything in public speeches, in their essays, and in their social functions to show their appreciation of serious actors like Roscius and Aesopus. Young poets like Asinius Pollio and Varius Rufus filed away at poetic dramas that were published for library shelves but never reached the stage. Critics like Horace wrote to prove that what the populace greeted at every change as a new and remarkable advance was nothing but a new step downward. And down it went. The drama in some form remained a necessity for the populace and they kept it at their level. The intelligent, who had in themselves, their companions and their libraries their own means of entertainment, deserted the theater which had grown unendurable to them.

CHAPTER V

THE PROSE OF THE ROMAN STATESMEN

"Ciceronian prose is practically the prose of the human race," says Mackail, a critic who is unusually sensitive to qualities of style. In saying this, he doubtless had in mind not only the orotund periods of the *Pro Milone*, the elaborately rhythmical movement of the *Pro Archia*, the vehement force of the first Catilinarian or the easy colloquialism of the familiar letters. It was rather the lucid and copious exposition of essays like the *De Oratore* in which, without revealed effort, a versatile mind found appropriate and dignified expression for all its concepts and moods. How did such prose come to be?

Cicero worked incessantly for years to acquire his command of the tools of expression. When very young he memorized the standard rules of rhetoric that emphasized the need for clarity, arrangement, conciseness, luminosity, and all the rest. Do such rules make great writers? On that point Cicero did not deceive himself. He knew that adults did not need them, but he recognized that schoolboys would save time by having their attention called to what practice would eventually reveal. Such rules might prove guide posts to intelligent beginners, but one has only to read the three books of the *De Oratore*[1] to discover that rhetoric was for Cicero a schoolroom

[1] Cf. *De Oratore*, I. 23; 52; 105; 146; 198; II. 50; 77; 100; 132; III. 29–33; 48; 54; 93; 226; *Ad. Att.* iv. 16.3; *Brutus*, 263.

crutch to outgrow and forget. Another device much
recommended by the Roman teachers of his day was
imitation, the study of the masters of diverse styles.
It is a method that has recently been employed to
good effect in the classroom for the awakening of
taste and sharpening of critical acumen. Cicero did
not scorn its use, but he knew too well that style
is personal[2] to attempt to acquire in this way a
garb that would not fit his own mental processes.
When he sought out Apollonius of Rhodes as a
critic it was not in order to adapt himself to that
teacher's mode of expression. He first decided what
his own taste and capacity needed, and what the
Roman Forum and Curia would require of him;
then he sought for the teacher who could best help
him by his criticism. His complete independence is
shown by the fact that he traveled long, trying one
after the other of the famous teachers of the east,
abandoning them one by one as soon as he discovered that they did not suit his purposes.[3] Cicero
did not impose the Rhodian style upon himself. He
made his own curriculum to fit his temperament
and sought out the tutor who could help him attain
what he demanded. This procedure seems to me
characteristic of the great Roman stylists. Cicero
and Caesar, Sallust and Livy, Seneca and Tacitus,
betray themselves in their sentence structure. The
secret of their expression will never be disclosed by
a search for their models nor in the rhetorical rules
then current.

The aim of this chapter is limited. It cannot
even attempt the important task of illustrating from

[2] *De Oratore* iii. 29–33; *Brutus* 202, 212, 276, 286, *Orator* 99, 143.
[3] *Brutus* 315, 316.

a study of Cicero the valid rule that style is the man. It will attempt only to sketch the growth of Latin prose up to Cicero's day in order to suggest how that prose became adequate to clothe the varied expression of so versatile a genius.

Roman, like English, prose developed its sonority, dignity, and rhythm in persuasive speech. As in England during the religious reformation, pulpit oratory molded speech, so in Rome, during the period of political reformation from Cato to Cicero, forensic contests in the senate house and at the tribunals transformed Roman expression. This parallel may seem obvious, but one offers it with hesitation because Roman oratorical style is generally supposed to have been shaped by the study of Greek rhetoric in the schoolroom. Quite apart, however, from the fact that true art is seldom amenable to the compulsion of precept, chronology militates against this theory. Roman prose had traveled far before it resorted to any guidance from Greece.

Like the English of Wycliffe, early Roman prose was formless. It merely followed the habits of unshaped spontaneous conversation. If anything was to be recorded with care, it employed the forms of art, that is, of verse. Naevius and Ennius wrote their chronicles in meter. Even Chaucer, who is so luminous in his verse narratives, becomes involved and at times almost incoherent in his few attempts to write prose, unless in fact he yields to the temptation of admitting rhythm into his sentences. But Chaucer is one of the last of the great writers to flounder thus. The Wyclifite Bible marked the be-

ginning of a religious contest that continued for
two centuries with more or less intensity, and
finally with passionate vehemence. It was a contest that, to many, involved a question of life and
death and to even more the problem of eternal
salvation. The gravity of the theme called for the
noblest possible expression, while the deep concern
of all classes, even the most ignorant, required
clarity and directness of utterance. The temptation
of the learned to exaggerate rhetoric into Euphuism
was immediately checked by the need of being
intelligible to the congregation, while the tendency
of plain persons toward colloquial formlessness was
checked both by the deep respect for the sacred
theme and by the high level of cultural taste among
the clergy of the time. We need not deny the great
influence of Ciceronian and Augustinian models upon
these learned men, and in Lyly's courtly group we
know how ancient rhetoric ran pell-mell into pre-
ciosity. But that was an aberration that affected
only those who had a thin message to convey.
When men are intensely engaged in saving their
fellows, speech will grow clear, and when these men
are at the same time persons endowed with great
intellects, their speech will take on dignity of structure and of sound. Before that contest English
prose had babbled thus:[4]

And in that country is an old castle that stands upon
a rock, the which is cleped the Castle of the Sparrowhawk,
that is beyond the city of Layays, beside the town of
Pharsipee, that belongeth to the lordship of Cruk, that
is a rich lord and a good Christian man, where men find
a sparrowhawk upon a perch right fair and right well
made, and a fair Lady of Fayrye that keepeth it, etc.

[4] Sir John Mandeville.

This sentence rattles on unhaltingly through "and's" and "that's" for a solid page before it falls down to a stop from sheer exhaustion.

After the battle was over we have the Authorized Version with its magnificent directness:

> The sun shall be no more thy light by day; neither for brightness shall the moon give light unto thee; but the word shall be to thee an everlasting light, and thy God thy glory.

Briefly, the parallel between early Latin and early English prose can be indicated thus. The prose of Ennius, like that of Chaucer, was very much inferior to his verse. Before Ennius died, however, the mighty struggle of statesmen had begun in the polemics of Cato, a contest which was destined to build up in time a dignified and versatile language. Cato represented the native, middle-class, agrarian population of Italy that feared the expensive and ambitious foreign entanglements which the philhellenic party of Scipio had incurred and hated the foreign culture which followed in the wake of philhellenism. Cato spoke incessantly. A hundred and fifty of his speeches were available in Cicero's day. He attacked the Scipionic group in the senate, in public harangues, and in court. And not only he but his lieutenants—and of course his opponents—had constantly to be on their feet. This was the beginning of the party divisions that led through the Gracchan reforms and through the debating period of the civil wars to the final defeat of the Roman Republic a hundred years later. The contest of words was as bitter as in the England of Wycliffe, Tindall, Cranmer, Latimer, and Hooker.

Here, too, the best intellects of the nation were exercised in the debate; here, too, the gravity of the theme and the demands of aristocratic audiences required dignified expression, while the constant necessity of winning the populace required entire clarity and lucidity of expression. The struggle was not indeed for eternal salvation, but it often involved the question of life and death, and always the future of the state. And from men like Cato, the Gracchi, Cicero and Brutus, the state claimed and won a devotion more intense than religion could. Thus there is a certain similarity between the growth of Latin prose from Ennius to Cicero and that of English from Chaucer to Hooker. And though Greek rhetorical theory and models were factors in shaping Latin prose, as Roman theory and models were factors in shaping English, it seems to me quite probable that both languages would have taken the course they did without those models, for both were determined by forensic expression, by great causes, and by intense devotion to those causes on the part of the most intelligent men of their day.

In following the evolution of Latin prose[5] we unfortunately have to deal largely with fragments quoted by later writers, and we cannot always be sure that these fragments are representative. For our purposes however they may legitimately be considered so. Before Ennius' time very few speeches had actually been published. Cicero had at hand an old oration of Appius Claudius of about

[5] Nettleship, *Essays Classical*, II, 93; Norden *Die antike Kunstprosa* (which seriously overestimates the influence of Greek doctrine on Latin prose style). Cicero's *Brutus* is the indispensable handbook.

281 B.C. and some funerary laudations, but he did not think either worth considering in a history of oratory. So far as we know, written prose documents before these were confined to laws, treaties, and meager official records. The fragments of the Twelve Tables (450 B.C.) are too scanty to afford any basis for judging style. Some of them are so wanting in lucidity, because of an ambiguous use of pronominal subjects, that a modern lawyer might readily manipulate them to prove any point. A few fourth- and third-century inscriptions from headstones and votive tablets[6] contain only blunt sentences which reveal chiefly an obvious desire to save the expense of stone-cutting. They do however show the native Latin word order and its fondness for the deferred verb. *Orcevia Numeri (uxor) nationu gratia, Fortuna Diovo fileia primogenia donum dedi.* This is of course a tendency in all inflected languages where the verb can be postponed till the subject and object have been visualized, since the inflectional endings indicate the direction of the verbal action. And in Latin, the hierarchy of *what is important* can be and was recognized by the word order. "Orcevia, Numerius' wife, for the gift of childbirth, to Fortuna, Jove's daughter the first-born, this gift I give." Strictly speaking Cicero's best-shaped sentence is not more periodic than that colloquial tablet of a humble woman a century before any Roman scholar thought of studying style. It was not the study of Greek that determined the form of Latin prose.

The Duilian inscription of 260 B.C.—doubtless authentic in the main though found in an imperial

[6] Cf. e.g. C.I.L. I. 60, 366, 561.

copy[7]—is our only pre-Ennian fragment of prose that contains several complete sentences. This inscription is far more fulsome and boastful than the modest Scipionic epitaphs of two generations later, a fact probably due to Duilius' sojourn in Sicily where he could see verbose honorary tablets at every hand. In spirit and content it is Sicilian, but its phrasing and diction are normal Latin. Its longest sentence is rambling, badly coordinated and illogically constructed despite its periodic placement of the verbs. The man who composed it had no feeling for lapidary style:

enque eodem mac [istratud bene]
[r]em navebos marid consol primos c[eset copiasque]
[c]lasesque navales primos ornavet pa[ravetque],
[c]umque eis navebos claseis Poenicas omn[is, item ma-]
[x]umas copias Cartaciniensis praesente[d Hanibaled]
[d]ictatored ol[or]om in altod marid pucn[andod vicet]
[v]ique nave[is cepe]t cum socieis septer[esmom unum
    quin—]
[queresm]osque triresmosque naveis X[XX, merset XIII]
etc.

[—and in the same magistracy he was the first consul to fight successfully upon the sea with ships, and he first equipped and prepared a fleet, and by fighting on the high seas he with his ships overcame the Punic fleet and the very great Carthaginian forces commanded by their dictator Hannibal, and by force he captured their ships with their marines, one septereme, and thirty quinqueremes and triremes, and sank thirteen, etc.]

A man who composes thus is not only "hypnotized by the exuberance of his own verbosity" but unpracticed in the art of logical expression.

Our first passage of continuous prose comes from Ennius' *Euhemerus*, quoted verbatim by Lactantius.

[7] The imperial copy is probably accurate except for a few words, *Class. Phil.* 1919, 74.

A fair example is the following:[8]

Exim Saturnus uxorem duxit Opem. Titan qui maior
natu erat postulat ut ipse regnaret. ibi Vesta mater
eorum et sorores Ceres atque Ops suadent Saturno, uti
de regno ne concedat fratri. ibi Titan, qui facie deterior
esset quam Saturnus, idcirco et quod videbat matrem
atque sorores suas operam dare uti Saturnus regnaret,
concessit ei ut is regnaret. itaque pactus est cum Saturno, uti si quid liberum virile secus ei natum esset, ne
quid educaret. Id eius rei causa fecit, uti ad suos gnatos
regnum rediret. tum Saturno filius qui primus natus est,
eum necaverunt. deinde posterius nati sunt gemini,
Iuppiter atque Iuno. tum Iunonem Saturno in con-
spectum dedere atque Iovem clam abscondunt dantque
eum Vestae educandum celantes Saturnum. item Nep-
tunum clam Saturno Ops parit eumque clanculum
abscondit, etc.

For this passage I shall use Professor Rand's
translation though it introduces a modicum of style
into the expression:

"Then Saturn took Ops to wife. Titan, his elder
brother, wished to be king himself. Then their mother
Vesta and their sisters Ceres and Ops induced Saturn
not to yield the throne to Titan. Then Titan, who was
not so handsome a man as Saturn, both on that account
and because he saw that his mother and sisters were bent
on having Saturn reign, allowed him so to do. He therefore secured an agreement with Saturn, that if the latter
had any male offspring thereafter, he should not rear
them. This he did for the purpose that the kingdom
might revert to his own sons. Then a first son was born
to Saturn, and they killed him. Then later twins were
born, Jupiter and Juno. Then they openly showed Juno
to Saturn, and hid Jove and gave him to Vesta to bring
up, concealing him from Saturn. Likewise Ops bare
Neptune unbeknownst to Saturn, and carefully hid him
away."

[8] Ed. Vahlen. Professor Rand's translation may be found in *Founders
of the Middle Ages* (Harvard University Press, 1928), 56.

This Ennian passage is even more simple and devoid of stylistic qualities than is the English of Wycliffe or Chaucer. The brief plodding sentences are clear enough; in fact there is a dry legalistic explicitness in phrases like *id ejus rei causa fecit uti*, and *deinde posterius*. But the whole rattles to pieces like a mosaic set in clay. It is in the main a string of coordinate clauses loosely hung on que, atque, ibi, tum, and without any appreciation of the differences that we attempt to convey by commas, semicolons and full stops. It has not even the normal feeling for periodic structure which the epitaphs of the time reveal. It is naive, primitive prose, and the evidence that Ennius could drivel thus is indeed illuminating to the student of literature. A nation which could be satisfied with such a medium of expression had not been very verbose.

During the next few decades, however, there was much legislation, and from the interesting Senatus Consultum de Bacchanalibus of 186 B.C. we have considerable fragments which prove that the ambiguities found in the Twelve Tables were being gradually removed and that there were enough shysters at Rome to compel legislators to evolve the intricate and all-inclusive "if-and-but style" which has ever since characterized legal expression. To this source the great prose of Rome owed very little except precision of diction. There was also not a little historical writing, chiefly however in Greek, for the use of statesmen who needed to know their precedents. But this type of prose, so far as we can judge from the fragments preserved and from Cicero's adverse judgments,[9] made no appreciable

[9] *De Orat.* ii, 51, 59.

advance upon the narrative manner of Ennius, illustrated above. Nor did such commonplace textbooks
as Cato's *De Agri Cultura*.

As we have said, it was public speech that
moulded prose style at Rome, as in England.
Among the first to make a marked impression was
Cato, whose great activity on the platform begins
about the year of the decree *de Bacchanalibus*.
Nothing could be more innocent of form than Cato's
De Agri Cultura. This however, is by no means
true of his speeches, several pages of which survive
in the typical paragraphs quoted by later writers.
Cato had not taken any course in the art of elo-
quence, he had not studied the Greeks to the point
of appreciating stylistic qualities, and there was no
literary Latin prose published for him to study, but
he had, as a member of the senate, heard many
elaborate arguments advanced by the foremost
statesmen of his day on such weighty questions as
the peace with Carthage, the proposed expedition
into Macedonia in aid of the Greek democracies,
the terms of peace with Philip, and the proposed
war with Antiochus the Great. There can be no
doubt that these debates brought out many of the
characteristic qualities of Latin style. The men who
argued these questions had to think soundly and
to form their arguments as clearly, as definitely, as
incisively, and as persuasively as they knew how.
When scholastic students of style attribute Greek
learning to Cato[10] because he stops to make defini-
tions, balance arguments, and employ logical enthy-
memes, they astound us by their naïvete. One

[10] As for instance Norden, *op. cit.* I, 164 ff.

might as well say that Confucius, Hesiod, and Isaiah had studied Demosthenes. Indeed I doubt not the Aurignacian mother defined words for her children and that the lord of the cave had often tried to argue his wife into silence by conclusions *ex contrario*.

There has recently arisen another explanation for the occasional artistry of the pre-hellenistic Roman writers which has been held to apply to all of the early Latin authors including Plautus. This is that the so-called "Gorgianic figures," used by even the earliest Romans, are of Sicilian origin, that the Romans must therefore have come into cultural contact with the Sicilians through commerce two centuries before Plautus, and that Latin prose may thus have taken on rhetorical devices in its infancy.[11] I mention these entertaining conjectures only to guard against any possible supposition that they may seem acceptable simply because they have found their way successively into recent textbooks. Cato was a man who, despite his faults, possessed a very keen and versatile mind, a visualizing, picture-making imagination, a sharp tongue, an agile as well as a retentive memory, and a penetrating power of analysis. His style, to be sure, is not malleable; the clauses cohere by logic rather than by the cement of conjunctions; he is repetitious, chiefly because he likes to hammer his nails firm; his transitions are blunt when he is impatient to be on with his argument; he does not take time to modulate his phrasing and his style has little *chiaroscuro*, because he is in deadly earnest all the way. His vocabulary is often of the barn

[11] Leo, *Gesch. Röm. Lit.* 37 ff.

and field and his imagery is apt to draw from the farmstead, as for instance when he shouts at Thermus: "You cut those ten worthy men into strips of bacon."[12] In his *Brutus*, Cicero somewhat slyly likened Cato's simple straightforward Latin to the style of Lysias.[13] Cicero, of course, knew the difference, for he later permitted Atticus to correct him on this point, but at the time he desired to recall Brutus to the logical consequences of a contemporary doctrine which somewhat naïvely overstressed the simplicity of the studied artlessness of Lysias. Cato was, of course, conscious of his effects; he drove his arguments home with intentional care, for he wrote out his speeches even though he delivered them without notes. He published them of course not as literary essays to be read by later students of oratory, but as documents designed to carry on the battles that he had begun in the court or the senate. Their art, such as it is, derives not from rhetoric but from his temperament and his fiery conviction. His philosophy of style lay in four words: *rem tene, verba sequentur*.

Cato's prose was admirably suited to forensic attack. Its qualities, however, were those that spring from a practical, quick-witted, imaginative debater. Cato probably directed every word and

---

[12] *In Thermum*. Tuum nefarium facinus pejore facinore operire postulas; succidias humanas facis, tantas trucidationes facis, decem capita libera interficis, decem hominibus vitam eripis, indicta causa, injudicatis, incondemnatis. The passage is packed with excellent examples of anaphora, balance, metaphor, homoeoteleuton and alliteration. Had this been written in 88 B.C. instead of in 188 we should take it as an excellent illustration of the result of Greek rhetorical study. It is, however, just native Latin speech afire with the most vehement Catonian wrath.

[13] *Brutus*, 67 ff.; modified in 284–6. Cicero had noticed that Cato's orations were full of imagery; *Brutus*, 69.

every clause toward the precise argumentative effect that he wished to obtain. He did not pronounce them slowly in order to taste their harmony of sound or to listen to their rhythm. If they had beauty, it was by chance or by reason of the beauty inherent in the Latin of his day. He probably deleted whatever created the impression of being far-sought. Spontaneous imagery might stand if it made his meaning more clear. His antithesis, anaphora, and balance therefore belong not to the schools but spring from the instinct to strike quickly, often, and with both fists. During his fifty years of strenuous speaking he did much for Latin prose, by proving that it could be clear, pointed, and precise; that it was adapted to senatorial deliberations over world politics, as well as to legal battles in the courts and in the assembly. Cato did not have an ear for the organ qualities of the language. Nor was the time yet ripe for the elaboration of artistic effects. When Cato spoke with deepest earnestness, he could hardly escape attaining to some of the dignity that Latin speech so readily acquires, but his vocabulary was too fresh from the soil to sustain that quality for long. However, it is likely that men of taste and restraint even in his day were more concerned than he for the proprieties of diction that belonged to themes of gravity. Nobles who were learning to rule provinces the wide world over and to give commands to kings did not have to go to Greek pettifoggers to acquire dignity of address.

Toward the end of Cato's period some nobles kept Greek teachers in their homes to teach their sons the language and the literature that prevailed in all the eastern half of the Empire. But the spirit of Rome was not then very friendly toward such teachers. The interminable wrangling of scores of Greek legations begging for favors, the disillusioning visits of Roman statesmen to Greek cities, the demoralizing influence of the country upon the soldiers stationed in Greece, the inane display of logical antinomies in the philosophical disputations, and the superficiality of a rhetorical doctrine concerned with adornments superimposed upon vacuity, these very quickly disgusted Rome. Cato's friends succeeded in having the Greek teachers banished from Rome in 161 and again in 154.[14] It would be as great a mistake to attribute lasting cultural effects to the ambassadorial visits of Crates and Carneades to Rome as to assume that the American senate could have adopted continental rhetoric and style from the exuberant prose spoken by the French and Italian envoys, Viviani and Francesco Nitti, who were sent to Washington in 1917 to present the cause of the allied nations.

After Cato's death more Greek teachers came, and among these the stoic Panaetius, who remained for some time and became a real cultural force in the group that gathered about the younger Scipio. Some attempt has been made to trace the Stoic rhetorical doctrine of the plain style to this contact.[15] But it is difficult to see what lessons Rome needed after Cato to illustrate the desirability of the qualities emphasized by stoic teaching: (1) pure diction, (2) clarity, (3) precision, (4) conciseness, (5) propriety. The first four of these qualities were the

14 Suet. *Rhet.* I; *Athen.* XII, 547.
15 Fiske, *Univ. Wis. Studies*, III, 62 ff.

very spirit of Cato's practiced though untutored Latin. The last quality concerned Cato very little in all probability, but other Roman statesmen knew the need of sloughing off barnyard diction in speaking before the august senators at Rome. Propriety of diction is after all a quality that could hardly be foreign to a people who had for centuries respected the triumphal garb, the fasces, and the august pontifical ceremonies, and it was not a quality that could be acquired from foreign teachers who did not know the tone of Latin words. We must also bear in mind that what Roman statesmen were eager to learn from men like Panaetius and Polybius and what these men desired to teach was not some clever trick of phrasing but the essence of political philosophy and of ethics. Polybius' sixth book and Cicero's *De Republica* and *De Officiis* are the real results of the early Stoic teaching at Rome, and Polybius' own unwieldy sentences should warn us that contact with Stoic teaching could do little for stylistic beauty.

As the Gracchan times approached, a new division of parties became apparent at Rome. The senators were suspected of promoting expansion in the provinces for the sake of their own profit and glory, and several tribunes gained popularity by opposing the recruiting and by haling nobles into court on the charge of maladministration. Piso devised the first of the special courts, which Cicero considered of great importance for the training of orators. Then for several years there was agitation over ballot reform advocated by the populace who desired a secret ballot. Many important speeches were

delivered in the senate and before the people on
these measures, and if we may judge from the
remarks of Cicero regarding Galba,[16] Lepidus Porcina, and Scipio Aemilianus, all this activity con-
duced to create a feeling for a smoother and more
coherent style. Aemilianus especially, who represented the finest aristocracy in its dignity of birth
and high accomplishment, spoke with that *auctoritas*
and *gravitas* that were the natural concomitants of
great empire.[17]

Then came the Gracchan proposals which shook
the staid government to its foundations. For a
dozen years the keenest minds of Rome were pitted
against each other, and victory lay not in arms but
in the power of persuasion. There was much discussion in the senate, but Tiberius Gracchus carried
the battle directly to the popular assembly, and that
is where it was fought to the end. For the words
of Tiberius we have to rely chiefly upon the paraphrases of Plutarch, which are too general to permit
of accurate estimate. From the speeches of Gaius
Gracchus, however, we fortunately have some exact
quotations.[18]

Gaius Gracchus did as much as any one man to
increase the range of Latin forensic prose. Reared

[16] Cicero, *Brutus*, 82, credits Galba with a lofty style in speeches
which somehow failed to survive in the written copies, which reveals
as in several instances that Latin style was apt to be primarily prag-
matic rather than scholastic (*ibid.*, 137, 138). To Aemilius Lepidus
Porcina (fl. about 140) he accords credit for smooth sentence structure
(*ibid*, 131).

[17] Cic. *Lael.* 96; *Pro Murena* 58.

[18] N. Häpke, *C. Semproni Gracchi Fragmenta* (Munich, 1915). This
editor finds a few instances of prose rhythms in Gracchus. I do not
think that Gracchus was conscious of them, since they occur in about the
same ratio as in Sallust or Caesar, who could hardly be accused of
encouraging the rhythmic style.

in the center of the dominant aristocracy where he imbibed the purest and most copious diction, trained by a mother whose urbane language delighted even Cicero, he nevertheless espoused the cause of democracy, and in the defense of this principle he acquired a lucid directness that Cicero never tires of praising. Gracchus had Greek teachers, who taught him to read and to speak Greek as well as not a little about Greek political ethics, and doubtless also the textbook rules of Greek style. Such stylistic rules, however, were not of much worth in addressing Roman voters, and they are seldom in evidence in the fragments which have survived. Cicero's one criticism of Gracchus' style is that he did not know how to modulate his prose so as to secure rhythmical effects. Gracchus would not have attempted to secure them had he known how. He was too concerned with the issues at stake, too fired with zeal for the cause for which he was to suffer death, to worry about the adornments of style. He published his speeches, and he doubtless prepared them beforehand, because in the revolutionary reforms that he proposed, errors of phrasing must be avoided, and the record must be kept for the sake of impressing his arguments. He certainly did not issue his speeches with a view to providing models of style.

In this period Latin prose acquired further versatility and range because Gracchus was a man of genius, believed in a cause which gave full scope to his great powers, and spoke before different audiences that required of him widely varying types of appeal. His was the task of shattering the power of the most stubborn aristocracy that the world has known, of organizing a new democratic machinery of government, of extending the suffrage throughout Italy, of saving the native stock by a vast scheme of colonization. He was stirred by an unflinching devotion to his cause, by bitterness at the murder of his brother, and by the knowledge that he too was marked for death. It is blasphemy against the informing spirit of great art to attribute his effects to rules, and not to acknowledge that genius fighting in such a cause is an independent creative force. Cato had already shaped his weapons for him. Gracchus, more richly endowed with vision, with sympathy, with intellect and wit, filed and hammered the weapons into a finished armory. There is no tool of persuasion that he did not have to employ. He used a simple, rude, staccato narrative when explaining before the rabble conditions that must be cured;[19] in elaborate argument, where the light and shade must be exact, he employed periods as well-packed, though not so musical, as those of Cicero.[20] Before senators his diction was as grave and lordly as theirs, while in the forum, though never coarse, he could be as colloquial as Cato. His vituperation carried the deep thrust of the lance rather than the rapier cut,[21] for he liked to play with lingering irony. His emotional appeal reminds one of the language of Ennius' tragedies.[22]

And yet Cicero was not quite satisfied with his speeches as works of art. What was lacking was after all what Gracchus would have disregarded

[19] Meyer, *Orat. Rom. Frag.*, 234.
[20] *Ibid.* 233.   [21] *Ibid.* 232.   [22] *Ibid.* 239.

even had he lived in Cicero's day: a more careful modulation, a studied use of rhythm, a concern for the collocation of sounds, a more elaborate sentence structure, and a more apparent contrast of light and shade. Those are qualities that do not belong to the expression of revolutionary reformers who have but a year or two in which to perform a great life-work. They must come with leisure and tranquility when men have time to try the sound and taste of phrases in patient reiteration. Meanwhile Latin prose had been fortunate in finding men like Cato and Gracchus to make it vivid, clear, versatile, and vibrant. After these two men and the scores of speakers that they drew into the arena,[23] no Roman could again write Latin with the shambling gait of Ennius' *Euhemerus* without serious apology. And it is safe to say that even writers of history and autobiography, who became numerous in the Gracchan period and after, comprehended now that sentences must have clarity, unity, logic, and precision.

After the death of Gracchus there was a temporary lull in politics; the victorious aristocracy, so nearly crushed, prudently decided to compromise with the populace rather than to risk the awakening of another Gracchus by exploiting their restored power. Young men who had heard the brilliant reformer in their youth, men like Crassus, Antonius, and Catulus, grew up to be distinguished orators.

[23] Cicero in his *Brutus* mentions fifteen speakers of the Catonian period, some twenty as being important between Cato and Tiberius Gracchus, about thirty who belonged distinctly to the period of the Gracchan reforms, and twenty more who gained distinction before the end of the second century; that is, some eighty-five whose contributions were worthy of mention before the fashion set in of studying rhetoric in Greece.

They inherited the results of a great evolution of prose, they directly or indirectly received the benefits of a deeper respect for elaborate style because of a new contact with Greek teachers, and they were granted the leisure and tranquility to consider the needs of a more artistic expression.

Licinius Crassus, in whose orations Cicero found the first mature Latin prose,[24] began as a partisan of Gaius Gracchus and in his youth doubtless imitated his hero's fiery style. He also gave some attention to the Greek rules though he held that rules did not create style but were merely a collection of deductions drawn by analysts from the practices of the eloquent.[25] He preferred observing Roman speakers to studying the precepts of the Greeks,[26] and he thought Roman oratory sounder than Greek because at Rome the pleaders were the foremost statesmen whereas in Greece only hirelings practiced the art.[27] In these views he was not far from representing orthodox opinions.[28] There were other great men who gave even less credit to scholastic practice. Antonius his rival—by many considered the more brilliant speaker of the two—claimed that rhetoric was useless in that it only formulated the

[24] Cic., *Brutus*, 161.   [25] Cic., *De Orat.* i. 146.

[26] Cic., *De Orat.* ii. 4. The few orthodox clausulae found in his fragments occur in about the ratio that one might expect in any normal Latin prose.

[27] Cic., *De Orat.* i. 198.

[28] In the year 92 Crassus attempted with his colleague Domitius by censorial pronouncement to discourage the growth of Latin schools of rhetoric. It is difficult to take seriously the recent hypothesis that this was an aristocratic attack upon democratic schools. Cicero's interpretation that the new Latin school was objectionable because it trained speakers without the cultural education in literature, philosophy, and history, which Greek rhetoricians usually required, seems adequate. Our own insistence that law schools require a college degree for entrance would then be analogous.

obvious;[29] Scaevola pointed out that Roman statesmen who had brought Roman government to the
pinnacle of glory had nothing to learn in expression
from inexperienced Greek pedagogues;[30] and Cicero's
account of the style of such great orators as Sulpicius, Caesar Strabo, and Cotta reveals the fact
that the oratory of these men was a home product.[31]

On the other hand there were men who tried to
make up for the deficiency in practical experience
by drilling at doctrine, with the usual result that
their language became tangled in artifice. Men like
Albucius[32] and the first Curio remind us in type
and experience of the courtly Tudor wits who had
little to do or say and ended in euphuism.

What was the admirable style of Crassus which
Cicero now calls mature? The samples that have
been saved for us by the *Auctor ad Herennium* unfortunately were quoted to illustrate vivid and rapid-
fire argumentation, and Cicero's longest quotation
was made to indicate Crassus' power of spontaneous
reaction to a surprising situation. While these examples give proof of celerity of wit, of a forceful,
picturesque, and copious diction, of the pungent
and concise phrasing for which Crassus was noted,
they are not normal forensic prose. They do not
reveal the dignity and harmony for which this
orator was praised, and they give no certain illus-

[29] Cic., *De Orat.* ii. 77 ff. Cicero, who dislikes to confess that good
oratory can arise out of native endowments, accords Antonius some
education, because he once conversed with the Athenian professors for
a few days on his way to the province! The *Brutus*, which attempts to
give genuine history, represents Antonius as a self-made man.

[30] *De Orat.* i. 105.

[31] *Ibid.*, ii. 88, 97 ff. *Brutus* 202, 276, 286, *Orat.* 99, 143, 214.

[32] *De Orat.* iii. 131 and 124.

tration of the prose rhythms that Cicero liked to find in a "mature" style. From the passages that we have we should say that Crassus spoke as a pupil of Gaius Gracchus, but with the mellowness of age and in causes of less moment.

Perhaps the real reason why Cicero found Crassus' style mature was that the Latin language was now mature. Latin diction had now become fuller and richer. Not only had the large bulk of Accian tragedy and of hundreds of comedies enriched the language, but hundreds of speeches delivered by men who had worked hard at the task of enlarging the resources of Latin phrase and diction had now been published. The special court instituted by Piso, the frequent cases before the plebeian assembly after the Gracchan period, the new custom of attacking political opponents by means of legal prosecutions had immensely increased the scope of oratory. The factional strife introduced by the Gracchans had divided the senate into debating groups, and brought fire into electioneering oratory and into legislative discussions. Every phase of political philosophy and expediency as well as of legal and moral principles was discussed day after day. Accordingly, the Latin language matured quickly and its prose was a finished product by the time that Cicero was born, although its verse had to wait another century before attaining adequate expression.

This prose was fortunately a fairly musical thing by nature. In comparing the earliest Latin word-forms with those of the Gracchan days we find that they had improved very much in musical quality, due in part, no doubt, to the fact that the Etruscans and Sabines, who had temporarily dominated Rome, had slurred over harsh collocations of consonants till they fell away, and partly to the fact that the plebeians, who were of course less conservative in speech than the patricians, had won great positions in the fourth century. *Jouxmenta* of the Stele inscription had now softened to *jumenta; stlis* had become *lis; stlocus*, locus; *forctis*, fortis; *scandsla*, scala; and so on, in hundreds of words. In many positions the harsh sibilants had been eliminated: *cosmis* had become comis; *dusmos*, dumus; and intervocalic *s* had become *r*: *eram* was better than *esam*. This elimination of harsh sounds had wrought so effectively between 500 B.C. and 100 B.C. that a language that was once as rough as Gothic had acquired the mellifluous quality of Italian. Though it still contained too many sibilants for ideal speech and the final *m* occurred so frequently as to invite monotony, it had few sounds that could jar upon the most delicate ear. The vowels were relatively pure, and because of the abundance in inflections of the sonorous vowels *a, o,* and *u* (= *oo*), they gave the language an orotund quality. The Indo-European *i* is on the whole apt to be shrill, and the great vowel shift of sixteenth-century England which altered it to the much more musical *i* (= *aye*) undid its benefit by raising English *e* to the thinner sound of the old *i*. Latin retained the old sound, but in *i*-stems it frequently went over by analogy to *e*, and the *āī, āǐ* diphthongs fortunately softened to the mellow *æ*. In all this, mechanistic forces of the speech organs were at work, but one cannot help thinking that a delicate auditory guidance helped select the desirable sounds.

Another great advantage inherent in the Latin language from the beginning was that quantities were carefully observed by it and were in fact the determining factor in its rhythm; and since time rather than stress is the guiding principle of music in human song, as in the flute and organ, Roman speech was to an unusual degree suited to modulated utterance. To be sure, in the century before Plautus, stress had threatened for a while to gain dominance in vulgar speech—enough in fact to question the rights of measured verse—, nevertheless the timely spread of the conservative, aristocratic pronunciation through political and forensic oratory, as it was heard almost daily in the open forum during the second century, gradually checked the process and standardized a precise observance of longs and shorts.

The emphatic dominance of quantity over speech went so far in controlling word-accent that about two centuries before Cicero it had drawn the accent to the penultimate vowel if that was long. Hence, in the sentence endings which so often consisted of weighty words, word-accent to a remarkable degree coincided with a natural quantitative utterance. Latin, therefore, lent itself to a rhythmical close of sentences, often combining word-stress and length of utterance in a way that Greek prose rhythm did not. Cicero had studied Greek and had observed that various writers advocated the use of iambs, dactyls, and paeans[33] for clause-endings, and

[33] *Orator*, 191 ff. When in *Orat.* 213 Cicero attempts to analyze the measures of Carbo his theory fails him. Again in 217, when he enumerates the feet that Greek theory allowed he fails to notice that his own feeling for Latin rhythms demanded a cretic before all of them. Indeed his selection of passages from his own orations in 210 is faulty (see Kroll's commentary). In fact his usage is far truer to the genius of Latin

he labored somewhat confusedly to justify those rhythms since Greek theory seemed to demand them, but modern analysis has proved that his ear had shaped a truer Latin rhythm than his scholarship or his logic. His favorite clausulae, though he was not fully aware of it, were cretics and trochaics, producing a rhythm that adapted itself excellently to the dominance of longs, to the penultimate law, and to a strong close. As usual, a true appreciation of the genius of the Latin language saved the art from the effect of rules that were made for another medium. Here again Latin shows its independence.

But this is not all. Cicero's books of rhetoric emphasize periodic sentence structure with careful attention to a mobile arrangement of clauses within the period. The Greek orators had of course practiced this art, and the teachers had drawn up the rules of the game afterwards. Cicero, for instance, often patterns his clauses with care in order to reach a periodic climax. In the *Orator*[34] he quotes an example from a speech of his own in which he follows two pairs of balanced phrases and a pair of clauses with a tranquil dignified close.

Domus tibi deerat? At habebas; pecunia superabat? At egebas;
incurristi amens in columnas; in alienos insanus insanisti: depressam caecam jacentem domum pluris quam te et quam fortunas tuas aestimasti.

than his theory. It is probable that Tyrannio, with whom he discussed Greek accents and rhythms during this period (*ad Att.* xii. 6, 2—about June 46) misled him. We need also to bear in mind Cicero's statements that the ear unconsciously operates in selecting good rhythms (*Brutus*, 34) and that the tendency to seek balance—a very old quality of native Latin verse—also produces rhythm (doubtless because of the paenultimate law) (*Orator*, 167, 220). Needless to say, what compelled Cicero to shape clausulae somewhat unlike those of Isocrates was the stress-accent of Latin operating under the penultimate law.

[34] *Orator*, 224.

In such studied prose as in much of our free verse, the modulation depends not only upon the measured clausulae but also upon the parallelisms of phrase.[35] It is the two-fold rhythm that we so often find in the Authorized Version, in Hooker and in Browne, before English writers knew very much about the classical theories of prose rhythm. Now the point that needs to be emphasized is that Cicero would probably have written thus had he never known rules, had he only used with his infallible ear the prose that came to him shaped by a hundred great speakers. For, in the first place, the periodic structure was native to Latin, as we have seen, from the time of the earliest inscriptions. That structure is natural in highly inflected languages where the verb can be deferred in order to make room early for the important words and concepts, while unimportant phrases can be appropriately subordinated because their inflectional forms keep them tethered in thought to their owners even though separated by space. All this invites the service of taste to provide the contrast and balance, to give light and shade, to lift and to subdue, and then to bind the whole between introductory subject and concluding verb. No speaker of taste, given leisure and rich diction, could resist the temptation of thus elaborating such a language as Latin. The sentence of the untutored Cato, quoted above, though lacking in modulation, reveals a structural form not unlike the sentence of Cicero just cited.

Cicero repeatedly calls attention to what he designates as the adornment of good prose, adorn-

[35] This in turn tends to produce measured prose rhythm in Latin, *Orat.* 167, 220.

ments associated in Greek learning with the name of Gorgias. These are the tropes, i.e., the figures of speech, and the schemata, i.e., the patterned expressions of sentences. But he also tells us, fortunately, that there were none of these adornments which could not be found in the works of untutored old Cato,[36] and that even unschooled rustics employed metaphor. We have already remarked how modern scholars have sought to explain their presence. Explanations are of course not necessary. Men used metaphor and simile in the caves of the Dordogne 20,000 years ago; language began in metaphor when the primitive savage first called a dog "bowwow." Half the words of any language are still metaphorical. When a Roman tried to find some expression for thinking, whether he used *puto* or *intelligo* or *concipio* or *cogito* or *arbitror* or *existimo* or *opinor* or *censeo*, or *sentio*, he had to use a figure of speech. Men like Cato, Scipio, Gracchus, Cicero became powerful because they had imagination, saw visions, and put their visions into their words.

The same may be said of patterned phrases. Native Latin verse, shaped long before Greek was known at Rome, was particularly fond of balance and antithesis because it was a verse that rested on parallelism marked by the strong caesura and bound together by alliteration. Such was the form of the early prayers and proverbs of the Romans:

Postremus dicas, primus taceas.
Pastores, pecua, salve servassis.
Eorum sectam secuntur, multi mortales (Livius).
Immortales mortales, si foret fas flere (of Naevius).

[36] *Brutus* 69. He adds that uneducated peasants often use metaphors, *Orat.* 81.

This old, alliterative verse operated with antitheses, balance, contrast, anaphora, and word-play. Cicero needed no more to go to the Greeks for such simple devices than Cato, and I do not think that he did. If he employs them with more delicacy and restraint, it is partly because he learned with practice that his own youthful style had been prone to over-use the obvious tricks of speech.

Cicero also calls attention to the Greek rules for the proper organization of speeches, which must have (1) their introduction, (2) their exposition of the case, (3) their panoply of proof, (4) their refutation of the opponent, and (5) their conclusion. To Cicero this is of course schoolboy stuff.[37] It might save time for a freshman to have these obvious rules of composition called to his attention when he begins, but Cicero did not for a moment suppose that an adult who has had some practice needs instruction like this, or that men like Cato and Gracchus and the hundreds of other statesmen battling with the shrewdest minds of Rome needed to be told that the peroration belonged at the end and not at the beginning of a speech. Roman oratory during its hundred years of progress had never learned anything essential from these precepts. Their purpose was simply to train the Roman schoolboy to observe the processes involved in shaping speeches. The mistake of our modern critics has been to suppose that such rules as these created Roman prose. Nothing in Cicero's writings or practices justifies

[37] *De Orat.* i. 105 *non Graeci loquacitatem sine usu neque ex scholis cantilenam requirunt;* ii. 77–84. Cicero made a summary of the rules in his youth (the *De Inventione*) but none of his speeches follow these rules closely.

that assumption. Roman prose grew to full maturity from native roots, in native soil, and with native nurture.

Ornate Latin speech reached its complete development in the orations of Cicero. To modern Anglo-Saxon taste the more elaborate paragraphs seem overwrought. Our busy courts and legislatures desire facts clearly and compactly presented. This has made us impatient of the style of persuasion in speech. When we have leisure for vacation reading we may resort to polyphonic or imagist prose in essays and occasionally in fiction. We still have a place for protreptic sound in well-written paragraphs, but not during business hours. That is the chief reason why some of the Ciceronian periods now seem misplaced. Another seems to lie in a difference of temperament in the respective peoples. If the Latins were in any respect like the modern Italians in their sensitivity to dramatic utterance, they may have enjoyed emotional persuasion more than some of the ultramontane peoples. The very fact that Cicero's manner so frequently carried conviction in the courts, in the senate, and on the public platform removes him to that extent from modern ultramontane criticism. But Cicero himself was in his day considered a moderate and urged strongly that elaborate prose must never be used except for themes that could carry its burden. He also knew that the study of rhetoric was for young students only and not for mature statesmen. When in the *De Oratore* he represented Crassus and Antonius as giving such elementary instruction to the young students, Sulpicius and Cotta, he carefully dismissed the venerable Scaevola as being too dignified to participate in such a conversation. His sense of propriety here reveals the true Roman attitude toward Greek rhetoric.

To be sure Cicero was himself somewhat imposed upon by the claims of rhetoric which Greek teachers had elaborated, or he would not have written the *De Oratore*—even with apologies. The erroneous belief was still current that some one some day might work out a real science of style. Hence he wished to make his contribution to that science by setting down his own precepts regarding prose rhythm, composition, and figures of speech. But that he had doubts concerning their validity appears in his insistence that the "grand manner" is a gift of nature (*Or.* 99) and that Roman oratory owed more to *ingenium* than to *doctrina* (*Or.* 143). However, in criticizing his contemporaries—Calvus, Caelius, and Calidius—he always proceeds from the point of view of their effect on him rather than from any reference to rules of rhetoric.

Cicero in fact employed few of the figures of speech, the names of which he felt that convention required him to list, and his modulations are so intricate and varied that, despite a score of dissertations on the subject, no one has yet succeeded in analyzing them according to the standard scheme which he transmitted from the accepted authorities. For Cicero himself, living prose had a native movement and a wealth of sound that lay beyond analysis. His rules were for dull minds that required the aid of rules. His own ear required none. The teacher who compels his students to count the specific clausulae of an oration of Cicero commits an unpardonable crime against the holy spirit of a great art. The student must, of course, learn to read that prose with an accurate pronunciation of the sounds and quantities, but after that the rhythm will take care of itself.

Cicero speaks[38] of his own oration *Pro Caecina* as an example of the "plain style," employed in explicative demonstration, and the *Pro Rabirio* as an illustration of the grave and lofty style employed in compelling persuasion, while he cites the *De Imperio Pompei* as an instance of the "middle style." He who has read these three speeches conscientiously feels the difference between them, yet he will not be able to convey that feeling by means of the traditional statistics of the stylistic doctorand. There are quite as many examples of the favorite rhythms (clausulae) in the *Pro Caecina* as in the *Pro Rabirio*, a fact that shows that Cicero's ear was remarkably sensitive to this effect and guided his vocal expression even when he was not consciously striving for it. Even in metaphors and in such devices as the rhetorical question, the *Pro Caecina* does not differ materially from the *Pro Rabirio*.[39] And this again shows that this orator was by nature luminous and aggressive as a successful speaker must be.

In the final analysis, if we may take the cue from these speeches, it is not the degree of consciously imposed rhetoric that differentiates their styles for Cicero, but the nature of the issues and

[38] *Orat.* 102.
[39] Gotzes, *De Ciceronis tribus generibus dicendi.*

audiences involved and the resultant quality of the speaker's inspiration.[40] In the *Pro Caecina*, an ordinary civil suit called for close argumentation before a small jury of legal specialists. These facts determined the style, as Cicero says. In the *Pro Rabirio*, which Cicero places at the opposite end of the scale, the critic will not find many more of the standard devices of rhetoric than in the other. But here it becomes apparent from the first sentence that Cicero is tense, that standing at full height he is battling with all his might for what seems to him a great principle. The issue was as serious as any he had ever championed. That accounts for the intensity of his utterance. But there are various ways of fighting, and the audience as well as the theme must determine the manner. Cicero had before him not only the voting public—which standing alone might have tempted him into mere vituperation—but he had also before him the aristocracy of the senate waiting to see whether the *auctoritas senatus* would be betrayed by that day's vote because of a possible failure on the orator's part. Cicero did not fail. The speech in its gravity and dignity of word and period is worthy of the theme and adapted to the audience. And these are the factors which Cicero felt had made that speech. Scholars have catalogued externals in such oratory too assiduously, and Cicero did so himself, because it had not yet been discovered in his day that art is beyond the reach of science.

What we need to do in reading Cicero is first to comprehend the rich endowment of the man: the

[40] *Orat.* 102 ff. and especially, *Orat.* 24, where he says explicitly: *eloquentiae moderatrix fuit auditorum prudentia.*

vast human sympathy that brought him into immediate contact with his audiences, be they ever so
diverse, the celerity of his thought, the constructive
power of his imagination, the close correspondence
between his delicate sense of rhythm and sound
and his copious vocabulary, and above all his very
sensitive response to the issues of right and justice.
Then we must bear in mind the breadth of his studies
in philosophy, dramatic literature, history, law, and
politics that enriched his mind with principles, illustrations, and points of view.[41] Finally, we must
picture to ourselves in each case the nature of his
audience, the issue at stake, and the intensity of its
appeal to him. When we have done this we shall
feel, if we have the gift of insight, and even if we
cannot analyze it, the consummate art of Cicero's
Latin prose. To attempt to express the secret of
it in statistics of tropes and meters is to miss it
wholly.

Before his death Cicero saw the fate of his
favorite literary creed that prose should be a work
of art. It is well to remember that as he had adopted
this creed from his teachers so had his literary
opponents adopted from their teachers at least the
verbal expression of their own creed, i.e., that it
was the business of the speaker to do the task
before him simply and honestly without resorting
to artifice. However, I do not believe that the literary contest that cost Cicero so much distress in
his last days was essentially one of theory; it was
rather one that grew out of the milieu in which he
lived. Long before Caesar's day, Cato had expressed

[41] Hubbell, *The Influence of Isocrates on Cicero*, etc. (Yale, 1913).

his natural aversion to the artifices of Crates and Carneadas when he said with his characteristic impatience: "Get hold of your theme and the words will take care of themselves." Cicero in his youth had found the same antithesis expressed in Antonius and Crassus. And he lived to see men like Caesar, Brutus, and Calvus win the young men away from his own ideals to those of the matter-of-fact style. The antithesis lies deep in human nature and crops up in the revolt that each generation feels toward its predecessor. It is hardly sound to attribute the dominance of such elementary creeds to schoolroom precepts. The preceptor is usually a man who notes the requirements of his day and tries to prepare his pupils for its needs. He follows more often than he leads, as any one may observe who will examine any twenty standard books on composition produced by teachers during the last fifty years in America. They follow usage, they do not beget it.

Asianic rhetoric, with its advocacy of adornment, had come to Rome in Cicero's youth. It is true that its rules engaged his attention. But a man as sensitive to artistic expression as Cicero, and as sure of the spirit of his audiences, had little to learn from Anatolian pedagogues who taught *Graeculi* how to declaim to four walls. Those teachers would hardly have recognized the *Pro Rabirio* as a product of their precepts. Similarly, Apollodorus came from Pergamum to teach the doctrines of a Lysianic or Attic style. Youths like Calidius, Calvus, and Pollio favored his method. But Apollodorus would have met with little success if so many Romans had not been practical and if the senate, with its traditions of dignity, had not already lost its prestige before the emerging democracy led by Caesar. Apollodorus may have introduced the new style, but had the times not been ripe for him he would not have been heard; moreover, the part of his doctrine that Rome accepted, Rome had possessed already in the 150 speeches of old Cato. It was Caesar's sword that antiquated senatorial oratory as it antiquated senatorial pretensions to govern Rome. Foreign schoolteachers did not do it. The Greek observer, Dionysius of Halicarnassus, who was an enthusiastic supporter of Atticism in the Augustan day, realized that it was not the Greek schoolteachers but the practical statesmen of Rome who in the last analysis required the new prose to take the form it did. "It is my belief," he says, "that this great revolution [in stylistic matters] was originated by Rome, the mistress of the world, who compelled entire nations to look to her: Rome, I say, and her nobles, men of high character, excellent administrators, highly cultivated, and of high critical intelligence." Here we have a keen insight into the fact that a powerful state generates a dominant culture which easily drowns the feeble whispers of the cloistered theorist.

The generation which followed Cicero, represented by Asinius Pollio and Messala, revolted completely against Cicero's ornate prose and adopted the plain, matter-of-fact speech which was called Atticistic. Again it seems to me not only incorrect but contrary to the penetrating observations of Tacitus[42] to attribute this revolt to the victory of

[42] Tacitus, *Dialogus* 19, 37, 38.

a stylistic theory. Calvus, to be sure, represented the new style in a few speeches as early as 58 B.C. when he was but twenty-four years of age; Calidius began to speak earlier, but whether or not in the new manner is unknown. Brutus, controlled by a temperamental bluntness, supported the same tendency a few years later. But these men would not have been able to undermine the power of Ciceronian style had not events worked in their favor. It was the dominating political influence of Caesar that did the work. The first blow was Caesar's quiet introduction of stenographers into the senate in 59. By publishing the minutes of the senatorial proceedings he compelled the speakers to consider the outside public, to drop the orotund periods addressed to their colleagues alone, and to confine themselves to pertinent details. Caesar himself had no time to waste on model orations. When opposed by the senate he carried his bills to the assembly to which he put his arguments in plain and pithy sentences. Cicero had scented the meaning of these effects enough to feel the need of stating his doctrine in full in the *De Oratore* published in 55, and Calvus and Calidius were quietly profiting by the new trend. Presently, in 52, the triumvirs closed the second nursery of ornate prose, by passing a bill which severely limited the time of pleas in court. The purpose was, of course, to expedite the business of the overburdened courts, but the act reveals once more that the new politics were concerned with getting results, not with encouraging a time-consuming oratory. Two years later Caesar crossed the Rubicon, and thereafter, so long as Caesar lived,

addresses in the senate all partook of the nature of
business-like reports in committees that met before
a curt presiding officer; and in the courts, whose
judges were now appointed by Caesar, persuasive
oratory gave way to a rapid estimation of facts.

Cicero was well aware of all this.[43] During the
first few years of Caesar's dictatorship he com-
plained frequently that there was no longer a place
in the state for his gifts, and that his influence had
wholly gone. However, hoping for a restoration of
senatorial rule, he decided not to yield without some
effort. He invited the most promising young politicians of Caesar's circle to take practical exercises
in political oratory with him; in 47 or 46 he wrote
a letter of gentle remonstrance to Calvus, the most
influential theorist of the "Atticistic school;" and
for Brutus, who rejected the means of artistic expression for reasons of taste, he composed (in 46)
a full history of Latin oratory in which he tried to
show that Caesarian administration threatened to
suffocate a great art, that the development of that
art during more than a century had demonstrated
the correctness of his own doctrine, and that the
opposing theorists, men like Calvus and Calidius
who had profited from events, could not by their
methods create an effective style. Brutus, who of
course comprehended the animus of the volume,
responded with little enthusiasm and avoided the
burden of arguing by asking for a more explicit
statement of Cicero's position. Cicero responded at
once with the brilliant brochure called the *Orator*.
But though Cicero sent out many presentation

[43] Cicero is well aware of the fact that the suppression of the old
political freedom was endangering style: *Brutus* 21, 324.

copies the book met with general silence. No one was interested in tropes and prose rhythm at a time when Cato was taking his own life as an offering to the dying Republic. For the next two years the business of state rested on the brief staccato orders of a tyrant. At Caesar's death the senate came to life again for a brief period and the fourteen Philippics reveal the enduring power of Cicero's oratory, an art that had been well-nigh silent for ten years. Then Cicero, too, fell by the assassin's sword.

Presently Augustus established the throne and once more offered freedom of discussion in the senate. But freedom had disappeared. Augustus' trusted friends reported his views in the senate and before the people in business-like summaries. Cicero's very name was anathema as that of a rebel to the new régime. Pollio and Messala, who represented the opposition to the unpopular style, who practiced the arts of brevity and directness suited to the needs of the new régime, were accounted the models of Augustan Latin prose. Ciceronian ideals returned in time to the schoolroom but only after the schoolroom had lost touch with politics.

CHAPTER VI

REPUBLICAN HISTORIOGRAPHY AND LIVY

The Romans, like all builders of empires, were avid readers and writers of history. Their first two epics were the stories of the growth of Rome; the numerous autobiographies of the Republican period were the political *apologiae* of public men like Marius, Sulla, Scaurus, and Lucullus, who had given all their time to the affairs of state; before Livy composed his great work, at least a score of historians had written bulky accounts, now all lost, of the whole or some part of Rome's amazing story. Now that we have only fragments left of that splendid historical library it is easy to fall into serious misconceptions regarding the ideals and aims of those who wrote the nation's history. To these errors the Middle Ages contributed not a little by canonizing all the ancient authorities so that when modern historical criticism came into vogue the reaction against authority went too far and skepticism overleaped the mark. Furthermore, a group of modern critics, who know little about the past, impressed by the absence of rationalism in the medieval writers, have invented a theory of progress which denies all intelligence to human beings who lived before the eighteenth century. A recent book, misnamed *The Making of the Modern Mind*, actually begins its account with the dark ages, thereby succeeding fairly well in creating an impression of consistent progress, but it wholly neglects the great civilization which had reached the heights and fallen before the period discussed. One might with equal fairness write a biography of Ruskin by ignoring his creative early period and beginning with his emergence from his mental coma during his old age.

As archaeological discoveries at Rome are confirming much of the tradition which Mommsen and his successors rejected, it is becoming necessary for us to revise our conception of the methods of the early Roman historians. We now know that in its essentials the traditional picture of a large and prosperous Rome at the end of the regal period is correct.[1] We know something of its extensive walls, of its imposing temples, and of its far-reaching commerce. We are gaining no little respect for Livy's conception of a strong Sabine element in Rome, of the participation of Latins and Etruscans in the revolutionary wars that ended the regal period, and of a temporary weakening of Rome in the early decades of the Republic, when the Latins gained their independent status and the Sabellic tribes threatened the existence of the Latin League. If Mommsen were writing today, he would certainly accept a large part of early political history, for he himself in his *Staatsrecht* rehabilitated much of the constitutional history which he had previously excluded from his volumes. I do not mean that we

[1] Inez Scott, *Early Roman Tradition in the Light of Archaeology*, Memoirs Am. Acad. in Rome, VII (1929). The archaeological evidence referred to in this chapter may be found in my *Roman Buildings of the Republic* (Rome 1924), and in an essay on the "Early Temple of Castor," Mem. Am. Acad. in Rome, V; a part of this chapter has already appeared in the *Am. Hist. Rev.* (1927).

are ever going to reinstate the embroidery of fictitious battle-scenes and long senatorial debates
woven from family legends into the accounts of the
early period. Livy himself, who has left us the best
account of this picturesque tradition, warns the
reader adequately when he explains why he has
freely included legend in the first part of his work.
But with the archaeological evidence before us, it
is now possible to estimate what knowledge of the
earlier Republican period was available to the annalists and to judge from this what use they made
of their knowledge. We know, for example, that
they had access to large collections of laws, senatus
consulta, treaties, and priestly annals, and that they
drew the correct inferences from the extensive remains of the city about them, a city which did not
greatly change its ancient aspect until after the
Second Punic War. The fact that in the attempt
to synchronize the consular list with temple records
which did not quite accord, they fell into a slight
discrepancy of a few years in the chronology of the
early period does not materially affect its value.

Various recent books on historiography[2] make
little or no reference to these revisions of our knowledge. They are being written as though nothing
had been discovered since Wachsmuth and the early
critical work of Pais. What is equally disturbing,
they continue to assume that Roman senators like
Fabius and Cato, who constantly had to consult
Rome's laws and treaties in order to direct senatorial
debate on intricate matters of international relations,
immediately forgot the value of facts when they

[2] E.g. Rosenberg, *Einleitung und Quellenkunde*, and J. T. Shotwell,
Introduction to the History of History.

undertook to write history. It is no longer justifiable, however, to group all Roman annalists together in one category. If the early annals of Rome tell practically the same story as the remains, there must have been a great difference between the statesmen who first recorded the facts and the romancers of Sulla's day who wrote popular books for the purpose of entertainment.

We may classify the historical writers of the Republic into three distinct groups with reference to their methods and their employment of their sources. In the century before Gaius Gracchus, we know of some eight statesmen who told the story of Rome from the beginning up to their own day. These are Fabius Pictor, senator and pontifex, who had served in the army in 225 B.C., L. Cincius Alimentus, a praetor and general in the Hannibalic war, Cato, consul and censor, C. Acilius, a senator, Postumius Albinus, a consul, Cassius Hemina, Fabius Servilianus, consul and commentator on pontifical law, Calpurnius Piso, consul, censor, and reformer of the courts, and Sempronius Tuditanus, a jurist, who while consul conquered Histria. They all wrote at a time when there were few "general readers," and their works were in the main intended for the information of magistrates, senators, jurists, and a small circle of readers closely connected with the ruling classes. These men were all thoroughly acquainted with Rome's' laws and treaties.

After the Gracchan revolution we find a decided change in the tone and purpose of history. The democratic upheaval had enlarged the circle of readers by bringing large masses into the political arena, and had created a demand for histories that were more easy to read and more sympathetic toward the aspirations of the common people. In addition, a diffusion of the knowledge of Greek, which made available the colorful histories that Alexandrian culture had produced, and which fostered a taste for a more florid style in written and spoken Latin, tended to turn readers away from the dry factitive annals of the preceding century and to encourage professional writers to satisfy the new taste. The first story-teller to meet the new demand was apparently Cn. Gellius of the Gracchan age, who seems to have filled in the meager outline of early Republican history with an abundance of interesting legends. The period that had been covered in seven rolls by the sober Piso required ninety-seven in the library that Gellius produced.

This feat marks an epoch in Roman historiography. Where Gellius found all his material we are not told, but we may surmise with some degree of accuracy. He seems not to have added much to the legends of the regal period, for even the earlier annalists had, with due warning to the reader, repeated the household tales of that epoch. Most of the padding appears in the section devoted to the first two centuries of the Republic. In this portion the older statesmen-historians had shown their restraint by excluding oral tradition and confining themselves practically to the bare statements found in the priestly annals and in the archives. Piso, for instance, gave only two books to the two hundred years from 500 to 300 B.C., an average of about twelve lines a year. He apparently adhered closely to archival material. Gellius devoted about twenty books to this period. To do so he must have consulted heads of old families and gathered up all the colorful stories they had to tell of their ancestors for the period before the Third Samnite War. After him Sempronius Asellio and Claudius Quadrigarius, although both were popularizers, nevertheless reverted to a conservative treatment of the semi-historical period, but Valerius Antias of the Sullan age, the most successful of the romancing historians, followed the dangerous example of Gellius. It seems to have been his ambition to retell in a more persuasive form all the more interesting tales collected by Gellius. Thereafter it was quite impossible to satisfy the general taste in history without including the legendary stories of the middle period. It was this group, writing for a large semi-educated public, and providing patriotic, dramatic, and attractive volumes—in which vivid pen-pictures served the purpose of modern colored illustrations—that destroyed the taste for the sober old annals.

During the same period and catering to the same taste, many histories of special periods and propagandizing biographies appeared. Caelius Antipater, a professional writer, produced a history of the Second Punic War in which dramatic composition and stylistic values counted for more than accuracy. He wrote not for the information of statesmen but rather for the delectation of the young and the leisured dilettanti. Some of the autobiographies and histories of the time were produced by important statesmen, but their value was in many cases marred by a willingness to cater to the lower critical standards of the day and no less by a desire to excuse their political behavior at a time when factional strife had raised dangerous animosities. Fannius, indeed, seems to have written with some sobriety regarding his part in the Gracchan struggle, but Aemilius Scaurus, Sulla, Marius, and Catulus pleaded their cases with more or less open partisanship. Of similar tendency, though more restrained, were men like Licinius Macer, Cornelius Sisenna, and Sallust, who, having engaged in the factional struggles of their day, wrote history with a political bias, and furthermore, heeded the new demand for stylistic attractiveness to the extent of disregarding now and then the requirements of accuracy.

The third group of writers, the professional researchers, appears during the Ciceronian period. As the first extension of a superficial culture had created a demand for easy and interesting general histories, so the spread of a more thorough education produced a class of readers who became suspicious of popular accounts and demanded solider works on special topics. Furthermore, the increasing number of writers desired reference books that presented details in more compendious and reliable form than did the voluminous histories of the Sullan age. It was in response to such demands that dry antiquarians now wrote their crabbed commentaries and encyclopaedias. Aelius Stilo, best known for his grammatical work, also delved in the sources of political history. Varro, his pupil, compiled reference books on Roman law, on religious institutions, on the Roman *tribus*, and on geography. The great jurist Sulpicius wrote commentaries on the Twelve

Tables and a history of the praetorian edicts. Licinius Macer[3] and Aelius Tubero attempted to find new archival materials in the priestly offices and financial bureaus, various men made up convenient *libri magistratuum*, and even Cicero so far entered the field of the specialist as to write a history of Roman oratory, in the preparation of which he read hundreds of orations. Such special studies naturally did not supplant the popular accounts—in fact a score of less serious writers were busy at the same time—but their influence upon historiography was abiding. Livy, for example, not only used their digests of material but learned from them to be skeptical of the Sullan romancers and to respect the data provided by the early annalists whose books were no longer in general circulation. Hence, while endeavoring to create a great work of art that might supplant the most fascinating of his predecessors, he also attained to a higher standard of accuracy than his rivals.

In this brief sketch of Republican historiography it becomes apparent that it is in the second period, the time of popularization and of Hellenistic influence, that the historical conscience weakened. We must now revert to the earlier annalists to see how they worked and to understand how it was that they succeeded in preserving the essential basis of facts that modern discoveries are verifying. The field covered by these annalists may be divided into three parts: (*a*) the regal period (largely legendary); (*b*) the first two centuries of the Republic (500–280 B.C.), for which some archival materials existed;

[3] See art. "Licinius Macer," by Münzer, *in Realencycl.*, XIII.

and (c) the period after 280 B.C., in which archival material could safely be supplemented by reports of eyewitnesses, partly Greek, and later by the native written records. Critics of the nineteenth century popularized the view that Fabius Pictor must have worked with unsafe conceptions of history because he told several of the early legends in full. This criticism misses a vital distinction which the Romans themselves recognized. The early annalists knew that the regal period provided no reliable sources, but, with due warning to the reader, they reported the legends for what they might be worth. Fabius[4] seems to have been rather meticulous in giving these exactly as he had heard them without any attempt to rationalize them, for Dionysius enjoys pointing out their unplausible elements. Where we must test the scientific attitude of the early annalists is in their treatment of the second and third periods.

As regards the second period, we have seen that Piso, the last of the group—whose statements are as full as any—has in this portion an average of only about twelve lines per year. There is for this second period no trace of legendary material in the fragments of any of the earliest historians, and we can well understand why Cicero constantly compares the oldest accounts with the wiry *Annales Maximi*, why Dionysius says that in this portion they touched only upon outstanding facts, and why

---

[4] Cato's first three books of *Origines* similarly recorded the legends of other Italian cities without pretending to judge their historical value, but in his history of his own day he proved himself a very accurate observer. However, he seems to have treated only episodes that interested him. Piso, the last of the early annalists, introduced the unwise method of rationalizing the early myths in order to make them more plausible.

Asellio complains that no annalists before him had adequately discussed the causes of the events which they recorded.

The archives had some material of value for the whole of these two centuries. The high priests' tablets of the Regia, though originally intended only as a record of sacrifices to be performed, contained many noteworthy items because the pontifex was usually one of the most distinguished statesmen and accordingly interpreted political events as of sacred importance. Each year's tablet included the names of the consuls, and contained references to the declarations of war, to victories, defeats, famines, pestilences, destructive fires, earthquakes, and eclipses, or other events that had called for expiations or thank-offerings. We are told that when the contents of the *Annales Maximi* were published about the Gracchan time they filled eighty volumes. Since the period covered was nearly four centuries we may assume on the average a volume, presumably of about a thousand lines, for every five years, or about two hundred lines a year. If only a tenth of the material was of interest to an historian these annals would still contain enough to fill the earlier books of a writer like Piso. In the Capitoline temple were stored almost all of Rome's treaties, engraved upon bronze or stone. Since Rome's fetial customs were carefully observed during the long period of expansion, these treaties provided a dependable record of her external history. Before Vespasian's reign, as we happen to hear, three thousand of these documents had accumulated. In Fabius' day, judging from the extent of Rome's federation, we may safely assume at least a hundred. In the temple of Saturn were kept the laws passed by the centuriate assembly, in the temple of Ceres the important decrees of the senate. There were also temple records, inscriptions upon public buildings and, furthermore, independent local records in Rome's various colonies, which in some measure provided a check for those at Rome. And finally the existence of the old walls and temples up to the time of these historians furnished visible evidence of what Rome's ancient culture was like.

We are, of course, constantly told that the Gallic fire of 387 B.C. probably destroyed the old temples together with their records. This is one of the assumptions that archaeology has disproved.[5] We now possess a fairly complete analysis of Rome's building materials and we have discovered that in almost every instance the old walls of the ancient temples remained standing into the late Republic and their materials—being consecrated—were used again in the reconstruction of those temples after the use of concrete had been discovered (about 150 B.C.). The original Capitoline temple with all its treaties survived till Sulla's day; the Regia, in which the pontifical tablets were stored, remained intact till after the tablets were published; the original temple of Saturn with its valuable archives stood till it was rebuilt after Caesar's death; the temple of Castor survived till it was rebuilt in 117 B.C., and we know from Pliny that Ceres' temple, where the senate's decrees were kept, remained intact till the Augustan period. If the Gauls spared the temples

[5] Some of the evidence may be found in my *Roman Buildings*, 53, 78, 83.

in fear of divine vengeance—the Celts and early
Romans were equally religious—they would probably spare the consecrated contents. There is no
longer any excuse for repeating the unfounded conjecture that all of the early Republican archives
were destroyed in the Gallic fire. The places in
which they were kept certainly survived and the
fact that the early annalists to a remarkable extent
stand the test of modern investigation indicates that
some of the archives also survived.

Whether or not such material existed in the
temples would, however, be a futile question, if, as
Mommsen held, the Roman historians neglected to
consult their archives. It is certainly true that after
the Sullan period we hear little of research among
original documents. But quite apart from the decay
of historical standards, it is obvious that the desired
materials were then largely accessible in published
form. After the Sullan day every few years brought
out new biographies and contemporary histories
which incorporated from daily observation the facts
of interest. Such sources became very numerous
and men no longer needed to go to the archives for
the kind of material that was wanted in popular
histories. Hence it became customary to turn to
books rather than to stored documents.

The situation had been wholly different during
the century before the Gracchi. Then published
source-books were just beginning to be made, and
there were no convenient libraries of extensive histories. There may have been an anonymous digest
of the priestly tablets before Fabius, but of this we
are not sure. A complete edition was not made till

the Gracchan period. An old code of sacred rules existed under the name of *Jus Papirianum*, and Sextus Aelius (consul in 198) had put out an edition of the Twelve Tables with a commentary and a list of the *legis actiones*. That was all. And yet senators were expected to know all the important documents that might be involved in senatorial debate. As Cicero[6] puts the matter in his *De Legibus* (III, 41), "It is necessary for a senator to know the commonwealth—completely I mean—to know its military and financial resources, what allies, "friends," and subjects it has, and the laws, terms, and treaties by which each attained to its position, and he must also know the parliamentary rules of the senate and the history of Rome." To attain to such command of the archival material in the early days necessitated much first-hand study and doubtless the making of individual digests. We are reminded of the medieval law-men of Iceland who conducted the "thing" in the period when no written codes existed and when they were compelled to keep all the laws and precedents at the command of their memories. Such senatorial practice was a preparation for historical composition which was very different from that attained by the professional writers of a later period. To assume that Fabius did not know the

---

[6] Cicero, like many a modern statesman, desired a favorable presentation of his deeds in history and biography. However, when it was not a question of his own deeds, his historical ideals were very high. In his *Brutus* (292–4) he insists that history requires the same accuracy as testimony given in court under oath. In the *De Oratore* (ii. 62–3) he says that the first requirement of the historian is to have courage to tell the whole truth and never to deceive. He consulted the archives even to get an accurate setting for his fictitious dialogues (*Ad. Att.* xiii. 33, 3; xiii. 3, 3; xii. 5, 3). Some modern critics have found heart to suspect Cicero's historical ideals because he insisted that history should be well written!

source-material because Livy seldom refers to original documents is to misunderstand the diverse methods that obtained in each man's day.

Roman historians of course knew the worth of Fabius Pictor. Livy went to him to check up extravagant statements; Dionysius refers to his conciseness and accuracy; Cicero, whose historical material in the *De Republica* and the *De Legibus* was based upon Fabius, vouched for his lack of rhetorical adornment, and Polybius followed him closely in the story of early Rome, in the first ten and last two years of the First Punic War, and in the Roman sections of the period from 241 to the end of the Second Punic War. The most meticulous of historians, Polybius, criticized Fabius only on the score of patriotic bias when giving generalized judgments on recent events. Polybius was of course a foreigner who could readily detect the nationalistic flavor, and after observing the aberrations of history during the world war we can readily comprehend that Fabius may have failed in objectivity in writing of the wars in which he took an active part. But there is no reason for supposing that he did not set himself a high standard in recording the actual events of Roman history.

Polybius has received very great praise for his insistence upon accuracy. Professor Shotwell[7] ends an enthusiastic chapter with the sentence: "But as long as history endures the ideals of Polybius will be an inspiration and guide." The praise is deserved, especially when we remember that Polybius had behind him in Greece nearly two centuries of

[7] *Op. cit.*, 201.

extravagant rhetorical history. But when we ask how it happened that he turned his back upon all that tradition, no explanations are offered. It is not an adequate interpretation to say that by living in banishment he was removed from the temptations of historians writing the story of their own people, for he usually succeeds in being quite objective even when he writes of the Achaean League. Is it not likely that his contact with matter-of-fact and legal-minded Roman senators induced him to adopt some of their manners and methods? His respect for the integrity, sanity, and uprightness of Roman senators of the Scipionic period he voices repeatedly[8] in contrasting their qualities with the unreliability, astuteness, and fickleness of his countrymen. It is also to be remembered that the first part of his history is based upon Fabius, who therefore was his first preceptor in historical writing. It would seem at least worth considering whether Polybius did not owe some of his qualities as an historian to the fact that he served his apprenticeship in history among the early Roman annalists and that he adapted his work to the public which had been brought up on those matter-of-fact books. At any rate he is well-nigh unique among the Greeks who wrote history after the classical period.

There is of course nothing to indicate that Fabius and his immediate followers were in any sense great historians. Without any literary background, with only such practice in writing as would come from composing state documents, occupied every day with the concerns of a rapidly expanding

[8] Polybius VI, 56; XIII, 3; XVIII, 35; XXXII, 8–9.

state, they recorded only public acts and public discussions. What men did and strove for, outside of the voting, legislating, and fighting groups, was not recorded. Not even within their chosen field does there appear a penetrative analysis of senatorial policy. Fabius, to be sure, enumerated the immediate causes of both of the Punic wars but only with a jurist's interest in deciding at what point the enemy had committed the breach for which he deserved punishment. As historians these men had the limitations of their qualities and of their occupations. But on the other hand there is no evidence that they knowingly garbled facts.

One may, then, be permitted to object to a common error of judgment regarding the nature of what is called the "scientific method" in ancient history. Students who have to deal with the gullible medieval chronicles seem to assume that historical criticism has but recently succeeded in creating a respect for objectivity and honesty in history, as though the logical processes of the mind were not fully developed in the human race twenty thousand years before the invention of the historical seminar. The incubus of religious authority dominant for centuries in the Middle Ages was a passing phase, as was the overweening respect for dramatic values in the Hellenistic historians and the eagerness to glorify families and the state in the Sullan romancers. But just as Polybius, when transplanted into a soberer atmosphere of action, rid himself with ease of the Hellenistic methods; as Julius Caesar, when occupied with absorbing actualities, could free himself from the habits of his day so far as to record

the very crimes for which he was being assailed by
Cato in the senate; as Ari Frodi in Iceland escaped
churchly influence sufficiently to write the history
of his island with the same respect for truth that
he used when judging a case at the "thing," so the
early statesmen-annalists of Rome, when recording
what was available for the historical period of the
Republic, employed documents and personal observations with the same meticulous care that they
used when presiding as praetors in the courts or
when as senators arguing cases of international relations. Their brief historical notes are largely preserved for us in Polybius, in Cicero's *De Republica*,
in Diodorus, and in the central skeleton structure
of Livy, and the continuous existence of these notes
in Roman times kept the legends from ever straying
wholly beyond the reach of actuality. This also
explains why it is that archaeological knowledge now
coming to hand is so frequently found to fit in with
what we have been wont to call "tradition."

The various currents of Roman historiography
united in the vast work of Livy, so that, Augustan
though he is, he may be taken as a typical product
of the several Republican schools. There is no one
formula by which the historian may employ Livy
without constant caution. Parts contain unadulter-
ated legend, parts that seem at first glance to be
sound record are based upon treacherous sources,
much is first-rate history; but who has the magic
flail that will shell off the husks? There is no more
insistent problem in Roman history than the correct
use of Livy, for he is, over large areas, our only
source, and over periods where he parallels Appian

and Cassius Dio he is generally so much sounder than they that he must be threshed through.

In estimating the quality of the thirty-five books extant[9]—unfortunately his early work and not the maturest product of his mind—we must distinguish between the results that are due to his own aims and capacities and those that are due to the nature of his varying sources. Everyone now admits with Tacitus[10] that Livy was scrupulously honest, that he was fair, that he did not permit himself to fabricate—as Caelius and Valerius seem to have done—and that he chose good sources when they were available; but a historian needs more than these virtues. What we miss most in this respect is his failure to go insistently to primary sources. To be sure, it was impossible for a man who set out to write a vast popular history—about three times the size of Gibbon's great life-work—to delve in the archives. Those documents were not then catalogued and classified as they now are. Cato the younger, for instance, when he needed an abstract of the treasury office for a relatively brief period had to pay his assistants some 30,000 denarii to have it made.[11] Ten times the amount would not have sufficed for Livy's extensive needs. He accordingly made use of what had been published, such things as the *Annales Maximi*, collected down to the Gracchan period, the magisterial lists as they had been revised by various hands, and collections of laws and senatorial decrees that had been made

[9] Cf. Klotz, art. "Livius," *in* Pauly-Wissowa-Kroll, XIII, 816 for a critical bibliography.

[10] Tacitus, *Ann.* 7, 34: *fidei praeclarus.*

[11] Plut. *Cato minor*, 18. On Roman archives see art. "Archive," *in* Pauly-Wissowa-Kroll, II, 560.

for the use of lawyers and law-makers. And some of these skeleton bones of history he took from conscientious annalists like Fabius and Piso, who specialized on such matters because they wrote not for the public but for members of the senate and the ruling nobility. Livy's purpose seems to have been to write a readable and full history of Rome which would displace the unreliable fictionalized history of Valerius Antias by being equally well written but far more reliable. But if he had insisted upon primary sources only he would not have completed one-tenth of his very extensive task. Given his aim and purpose, his duty was to find and exploit the best published documents and histories for each period, and with very few exceptions this is what he did.

It was also his purpose—which a modern historian might well deny himself—to set down the early legends of Rome. Here there were no historical sources, and the question was whether to omit the legends—as Mommsen has done—because they could not be considered worthy of credence, whether to rationalize them and attempt to rescue a kernel of fact as Piso did, and as Pais and Beloch have recently attempted to do, or finally to set them down as found, with a warning that they were legends. Mommsen's method was facile but we are glad that Livy did not use it. The legends are good literature; they also have a great value in revealing the temper of those who accepted them and passed them to future generations as worth having. Finally they prove upon comparison with archaeological facts to have a sounder basis in fact than Mommsen thought. Even if all their details be legendary, they represent a Rome that could not have been far from the actual state. In fact they prove to be nearer the actuality than the strange and lifeless civilization that Mommsen reconstructed for the early period out of unscientific etymologies and stereotyped conceptions of late legal institutions.

We are also glad that he did not follow Piso's lead in trying to use them "critically." Had he done so he would have transmitted them in garbled form and spoiled them, and won nothing in the process. We have learned from recent attempts that this method is a failure. A Charlemagne reconstructed from medieval French epics or a Theodoric shelled out of the Diedrek legend would at best not be accurate history. Thirty years ago our hypercritical historians tried it, and moved all the early dates of Roman history down a century or two. Archaeology has at least proved this a mistake, and we now are moving the dates back and most of the critics have got into the moving van. After all is said Livy's method was the soundest. His procedure was the more nearly scientific. It is with exceeding good sense that he says in his preface: "The early stories regarding Rome's foundation that are handed down to us in poetic romances rather than in sound historical records it is not my intention to support or to refute." And again in the preface of the sixth book he warns us that very nearly all that he had written in the preceding five books—up to the burning of Rome in 387—rested not on acceptable records but on legend. And even thereafter, throughout his work, whenever for any incident he is limited to the authors who employed legend he is quick to warn the reader of the nature of the source. These passages show that Livy was a sounder critic of Rome's legends than Polybius was in respect to Homeric stories. Historians who scold Livy for his preservation of legends have not only missed their value but have misunderstood Livy's cues.

We have perhaps a fairer quarrel with him for following the Greek custom of inserting fictive speeches in the body of his work. To the modern reader many of them are tedious and create a suspicion of being unreliable. It is never quite safe to quote a line from these speeches as indisputable evidence on any event, though most of them contain the gist of an actual speech delivered on the occasion stated. All we can usually be sure of is that they give Livy's conception of what was likely to have been said by the speaker in the situation. That is often worth having, for Livy usually knew more of the pertinent conditions than we do and he possessed a sympathetic penetration into pristine characters and events that enabled him to make valuable reconstructions. One has only to read the several speeches attributed to Scipio Africanus to see that they make a consistent and vivid portrait. If we have the patience to read these speeches with Livy's purpose in mind we shall know how to profit by them. The convention was of course understood, and was no more misleading than the equally artificial convention of modern historians who employ a kind of fictional mind-reading, a "stream of consciousness" device, which may be found on almost any page of Mommsen or De Sanctis. Mommsen could hardly have made a silent character like Caesar real without constantly conjecturing as to his intentions and motives, as when he writes: "Evidently here too it was Caesar's intention," or again "When Caesar projected the plan for a new code, it is not difficult to divine his intentions" (and he puts down a page of divining), or again, "So far Caesar might say that his object was attained." These musings of a great historian of our time are cast in a different form from the invented harangues of Livy and the Greeks, but we read them with the same caution, knowing that they are surmises. The historian, who like Livy and Mommsen must deal with tantalizingly fragmentary sources, must have the liberty to bridge the lacuna by some such method. But we will be on our guard when reading such matter.

Thus far I have spoken of Livy's work as affected by his aims and methods. What is even more important for the reader who uses Livy is to comprehend the varying quality of the available sources. For the long period before 200 B.C. there was of course no writing of history at Rome. Very meager records existed for most of the obscure period, 500–280, and these had been exploited by Fabius, but they made no story that could be told in a consecutive form. Hence their data were welded together with the help of legend during the second century before Christ. Of the story of the Samnite wars the mere skeleton is all we can accept as firm history. And that was as true before Livy wrote as after. Neither he nor anyone else could mend matters. For the Pyrrhic and First Punic War the sources were good but the corresponding part of Livy is lost. For books 21–30 the sources were full. Here two responsible participants, Fabius and Cincius, told the story from the Roman viewpoint, while three companions of Hannibal told the same story as they saw it from the Punic camp.[12] Any tendency to exaggerate on either side could at once be checked from the reports that came from the other, and the excellent Greek historian Polybius came soon after and did a great deal of checking. Here Livy had only to be diligent, fair, and honest to be able to write reliably. The third decade of Livy is accordingly as dependable history as we have of any ancient war. It is only in the brief Spanish portion, for which there was no Punic account, and where Polybius himself had written too enthusiastically of Scipio's work, that we touch quicksands.

Books 31–45 are not quite so firm. The chief difficulty here is that there was no contemporaneous historian at Rome for this period except Cato, who wrote a very brief account of a part of it. Polybius was the first to compose the whole story, but excellent as he was, he came some years after the events, had observed, so far as he did, only from his home in Greece, depended largely upon biased Rhodian writers, and knew so little about Rome's activities outside of Greece that he omitted much, in fact all of Rome's internal and western history. Campaigns in Gaul and Spain, for instance, did not get recorded at all until they were well permeated

---

[12] Silenus, Sosylus, and Chaireas; Eumachus of Naples may also have been a contemporary. The explicit details of the battles in Campania may well owe something to him.

with legend, and there was no account available from the opponent's side. Hence it is that here Livy is of necessity exceedingly uneven, treading on a fairly firm corduroy for most of the important events in Greece, but on a marshy ground of semi-legend when he has to deal with western campaigns. Fortunately the somewhat scanty documents of the state archives had been well culled before him by reliable men like Piso, and these usually kept the legends from dangerous extremes. It is a complete misunderstanding of Livy to suppose that he did not know the weaknesses of Valerius Antias when he used him. Livy knew them all along, but in some portions of this period he had no good source, had nothing available but Valerius and his kind, who had set things down as they heard them, fables and all. Livy's frequent citation of Valerius Antias does not betoken a gullible love of this writer, but is intended as a danger signal. Here there are several boggy spots. But fortunately the period deals largely with eastern affairs and for that portion the sources were fairly good. It is fair to say that Livy did as well as was to be done in his late day with the material and time available, and that nine-tenths of this portion is acceptable history.

The difficulties that an author of Livy's day had in dealing with the source-materials may be illustrated by a few examples. Hannibal's famous route over the Alps is still being discussed, though Hannibal had with him on the journey three Greek reporters who described it. Since they had no maps and no compasses, and names of rivers, tribes, and mountains had little interest for them, their accounts were so confused that Polybius and Caelius, who used them, fell into hopeless confusion. Their routes are quite impossible despite the fact that Polybius claims to have searched for the pass. Livy's route (from the mouth of the Iserè, to the headwaters of the Durance, thence across the passes and down to Turin) betrays lack of autopsy, but it is apparently based upon an identification of place-names mentioned in the sources by the use of some map of the Allobrogic country made, presumably, during Caesar's campaigns. Thus by using geographical knowledge recently attained he was able to hit upon a very probable solution that was hidden to earlier writers.

In my second illustration, the account of the Scipionic trials, Livy was less successful.[13] His record of the court procedure in the cases in the 38th book is confused in the extreme; but it is doubtful whether the facts were any longer available. No historian was writing at Rome at the time of the impeachments, and even if there had been one he probably would then have omitted mention of them as being outside the true province of political history. Even Polybius, who was devoted to the fame of the great Scipio, did not give any account of the trials, merely referring to them casually when giving a brief character sketch of Scipio. Nor would there have been any records in the archives, since the trials were not completed and the archives kept only the results of completed decisions. Finally, the affair fell at a time when it was not yet generally customary to publish speeches.

[13] Livy, 38, 50.

The two or three that Livy found seemed to be of dubious authenticity and were harangues that gave but few cues to the real facts. In fact no historian wrote up the affair until long afterwards, when partisan legends, some favorable to the Catonian position, and others to the Scipionic view, had obscured all the facts. It seems today that Livy yielded too much to the pro-Scipionic accounts, thereby undervaluing the opposite views, and many attempts have been made to amend him with the aid of an excursus which he inserted—perhaps in a second edition—and with the help of various casual references. In this affair the facts are now beyond reach and probably were so in Livy's day. Here, then, Livy did not follow hazy sources from choice. There were apparently no accurate records of the affair available. They were all late, and packed with hearsay partisanship.

Finally, we may well take an instance in which political custom and psychology were misunderstood by his predecessors so as to mislead Livy as well. The Second Macedonian War was brought on by a number of motives: fear of Philip, a desire for revenge, an enthusiasm for the Greek republics which were being oppressed, and other similar factors. The declaration, as such declarations usually are, emphasized not the important psychological imponderables but "the obligations of Rome to her allies." Now in point of fact there was no legal obligation that had to be heeded, and the states to be aided were *amici* but not permanent *socii*. But before any Roman historian—it was fifty years later—undertook to record this war and enumerate its causes the distinction between *amici* and *socii* had been virtually obliterated and the writers listed the several states as *socii*, though in a strict sense they were not. Had Livy tested these historians by reference to the original treaties in the record office he might have found reason to distrust them. But this of course was not his task. Now it cannot be done, but it seems probable that in this case the historians who first recorded the events were so far removed from them that they failed to comprehend the precise factors that caused that war, explained it in terms comprehensible in their day, and thus misled Livy.

It is my belief that modern emenders and critics who have not sufficiently studied the various sources of Livy have gone too far in assuming that Livy is untrustworthy in any and every portion of his work. When the necessary distinctions have been made we shall learn to use him to better advantage. De Sanctis[14] has shown that Livy's much criticized account of Hannibal's march on Rome in 211 B.C. is more reasonable than that of Caelius. Livy's account of the battle of the Trebia, which was formerly pronounced impossible, becomes lucid if we correct our conceptions of the early geography of the region of Placentia.[15] In 1926 while Beloch was pronouncing the Livian tradition of the third-century Fasti impossible, an Italian scholar was publishing a newly discovered fragment which proved the tradition correct. Beloch had to retract in an appendix of his volume.[16] Editions of the fourth decade of

[14] De Sanctis, *Storia dei Romani*, III, 2, 338 pp.
[15] See *Jour. Roman Studies*, 1919, 202.
[16] Beloch, *Röm Geschichte*, 89, 629.

Livy have regularly tampered with a reference to the building of the Apollo temple in 179 B.C. because they supposed the temple was earlier. A recent examination of the materials of the temple proves Livy's text correct. We now accept Livy's statement of Hannibal's march over the Alps as preferable to that of Polybius, as we know that his topography of New Carthage is better though Polybius had visited the place. By a simple emendation of one word Conway has revealed that Livy was correct about Hannibal's route into Etruria, though the account has been severely criticized for a century. With Kromayer we also accept his topography of the battle of Cannae and of Metaurus. And so the work of recovery continues. The day is approaching when we shall be able to give Livy his due for a good method, for honesty, and for fairness, as well as for a lucid style.

CHAPTER VII

CICERO'S RESPONSE TO EXPERIENCE

A shelf of books has been written upon the Greek sources of Cicero's ideas, and if one were to discuss the manner in which Cicero's own experiences modified those ideas before he accepted them for his own use one would ask for a second shelf of at least equal length. Cicero's political works, like the *De Republica* and the *De Legibus*, were written after an extensive perusal of Greek political masterpieces, but they are not, like many of the philosophical essays, paraphrases. The author betrays the fact that he has been in politics for a long time, that he has in fact been a party leader and has held the highest offices of state. He does deference abundantly to Plato, Polybius, and Panaetius for good suggestions, but it is an experienced Roman statesman who has the last word on every issue at stake.

Cicero's various political works are not all in agreement with each other nor with the utterances upon the same themes found in his letters and orations, nor do his political acts follow an unbending course. He lived in fact through a long period of revolutionary changes in politics, when consistency through a life-time would have betokened either inability to learn or stubborn intransigence. Drumann set him down as a turncoat, a judgment which Mommsen reiterated in a great variety of phrases.

Heinze, in a mistaken attempt to rescue Cicero's reputation, tried to prove that he had been a fairly consistent conservative through life. Zielinski, on the other hand, endeavored to show that Cicero's theories could be traced to his reading, and that a search in these sources would explain Cicero's somewhat wavering course.

All these views seem to me to emerge from cloisters that are very far removed from the kind of democratic politics that Cicero lived through, a kind of politics not entirely unfamiliar to some of us from daily observation. Drumann and Mommsen wrote in an atmosphere where firm and consistent loyalty to the existing régime was expected of all gentlemen and where firm independence and detachment were taken as marks of vacillation; and even Heinze's apology breathes some of the same spirit.[1] As for Cicero's dependence upon the theories of his predecessors, it must be admitted that no Roman knew them better or received more from them. But professors who delve in books all their lives are apt to over-estimate the effect of written theory and of tralatician ideas, and to under-estimate the momentum of facts that compel practical men to take quick and unpremeditated action. Very often Cicero saw the value of an idea in Plato or Panaetius only after an experience of his own had thrown him pell-mell upon the realities that disclosed the meaning of their abstract ideas. I wish here very briefly to outline his changes in political thought against the background of his experience and his reading.

[1] The prefaces of Tyrrell and Purser, and the brief biographies of Strachan-Davidson and of Boissier are models of sane judgment regarding Cicero's political behavior.

In speaking here of Cicero's party affiliations we must recall that political parties remained rather amorphous at Rome, since all citizens could cast their votes directly in the legislative assemblies without using representatives elected by means of well-organized party machinery; since labor, confined largely to slaves, had no voice in politics, and finally since commerce and industry, which are usually very powerful factors in legislation, never became strong enough at Rome to formulate an effective program. In the fourth century B.C. the plebeians had struggled to win political equality with the patricians; in the second century an era of good feeling reigned in which Polybius was aware only of a well-balanced coordination of functions between the executive, senate, and popular assembly acting in self-restrained rivalry; after the Gracchi the party issues, when at any time they became acute, could usually be formulated in terms of the question whether the assembly was sovereign or whether the aristocratic senate had the right to direct or check its operations. The special questions that arose during the period and that invited a frequent shifting of party loyalties were numerous, as for instance, the disposal of public lands, the constitution of the law-courts, the enfranchisement of the allies, the special ambitions of men like Marius, Sulla, Caesar, and Pompey, the power of the tribunate, and the legality of the *senatus consultum ultimum*. During this period the knights, the propertied middle-class, were usually found to be aligned on the democratic side because they could more readily secure what they desired by such a coalition; but whenever the populace showed an inclination to threaten the rights of property they quickly shifted toward the senate.

Cicero's father was a knight from the municipality of Arpinum, and a neighbor and distant relative of Marius. The old gentleman had marked leanings away from the theories of pure democracy; nevertheless in practice his relationship with Marius, his residence in a municipality where sympathies with the Italian allies begging for the franchise were strong, and his status as a knight were factors that at times drew him toward democracy. It is not surprising therefore that the young Cicero was placed in tutelage under Scaevola the augur, one of the liberal senators who presently showed his courage by refusing to vote Marius a traitor at Sulla's orders. We can also comprehend why the young student eagerly followed the speeches of Sulpicius, the tribune who tried to secure a practical franchise for the Italians, and in order to do so placed Marius in command of the army by removing Sulla. In the years 88–7 it is clear that Cicero lived in a very liberal atmosphere where optimate politics were not in favor. During the domination of Cinna, Cicero, who was then diligently studying philosophy, took no active part in politics, but it is apparent from his later judgments that he bore no love for this brutal leader of the democracy,[2] though the knights in general continued to support him. On the other hand, when Sulla returned, seized the dictatorship and executed sixteen hundred knights, Cicero ac-

---

[2] Throughout his life Cicero found no good word for Cinna, though he was fair enough to democracy to praise the Gracchans even during Sulla's ascendancy, *De Invent.* 1. 5.

quired for this aristocratic leader an aversion that left its mark throughout all his later writings. Through these years of revolution, therefore, Cicero's sympathies were determined chiefly by antipathy to the respective leaders of both extremes rather than by any party allegiance.

But when the courts were finally revived in the year 80, Cicero soon appeared in the defense of Roscius, whom no speaker of distinction had dared defend because a creature of Sulla had suborned the attack upon him. We may freely admit that Cicero did not take this case in order to reveal the venality of Sulla's régime. He would have betrayed his client if he had used this opportunity to attack Sulla, for he spoke before a jury of senators. It is of course quite apparent that if up to this time Cicero had been an outspoken opponent of the aristocracy, the friends of Roscius would not have risked employing him in the presence of that jury. But it is equally certain that Cicero would not have taken a case that was sure to lead to the exposure of Sulla's favorite, Chrysogonus, if he had been a confirmed follower of Sulla. In the speech he made one definite statement of his political sympathies: "Those who know me, know . . . . that, after the peaceful settlement, which I especially desired, could not be consummated, I favored the victory of the side that has conquered." This admission, that Sulla was not his first choice, made before a jury of senators at a time when few men dared speak against Sulla, can hardly be used to prove Cicero a supporter of Sulla. It is in fact clear evidence that his disapproval of Sulla's use of mil-

itary force was so well known that it had to be
admitted in court and, for the sake of his client,
excused so far as possible by an emphasis upon a
later course of acquiescence. The peroration of the
speech, a very courageous exposure of the brutalities
of the Sullan régime, which gives evidence of a
keen insight into social psychology, proves that
Cicero fully understood the evils of the dictatorship.

> There is not one among you who does not comprehend
> that the Roman people, formerly humane even in the
> treatment of enemies, is now suffering from a wave of
> cruelty here at home..... This not only has resulted in the
> utterly brutal murder of many citizens, but has destroyed
> in our people, once so compassionate, the capacity to feel
> any pity.[3]

When we consider these two passages in connection
with the fact that Cicero—without pay of course—
took a case which none of the distinguished men of
his day dared touch, we can only reach the conclusion that Cicero's aversion to Sulla and his crew
was at this time the dominant influence in his life.
This does not indeed prove Cicero a democrat, but
it does go far to explain why Cicero did not for
the next sixteen years reveal any sympathy for the
senatorial cause, and why during that period he frequently criticizes Sulla and his policies,[4] while men-
tioning the Gracchi in terms of high praise.[5] Cicero
was still a moderate liberal.

Cicero was in Greece when Sulla died and therefore had no share in the abortive revolution of

[3] *Pro Roscio*, 136.

[4] *In Caecil*, 70; *In Verr*. i. 37; iii, 81; *Pro Caec*. 69; *Pro Cluent*. 151;
In Toga Cand., ed. Stengl., 68; *Lex Agr*. ii. 81.

[5] *Pro Cluent*, 151; *In Toga Cand*. 69; *Lex Agr*. ii, 10; 31; *Pro Rab*.
14, 15. In the days of his most pronounced sympathy for the senate
he refers to the Gracchi with less deference and at times goes so far as
to justify their execution.

Lepidus. On his return he took few political cases, giving a large part of his time to practice in civil cases (Verr. II, 181), through which he won enough distinction to secure election to the questorship and aedileship.

In the first Verrine oration Cicero inveighed bitterly against the past venality of the senatorial courts, instituted by Sulla, and the selfishness of the oligarchy. This was of course in part due to his plan to frighten the jurors into a severe judgment, for he went on to remind them that a reform of the court had been proposed and indeed was probably imminent. However, it is clear that Cicero was eager to take the onerous case. He fought for the privilege, he spent months of expensive and unpaid effort in the midst of the canvassing season upon it, he went out of his way to reveal the sins of the senatorial misrule of the provinces, and to speak with high respect of democratic heroes like the Gracchi, and of democratic proposals like the return of the tribunate. All these things prove that Cicero could not at this time have been considered a supporter of the aristocracy. The equestrian order, with which he was still closely identified despite his entrance into the senate, had strongly supported Pompey and had united with the populace in electing him on a moderate democratic program. There can be no doubt that Cicero had voted wholeheartedly for Pompey and that he supported the equestrian-democratic *bloc* and program. If in the Sullan days he was an independent liberal with aversions to both Cinna and Sulla, he was now willing to work with the liberal group, even if a somewhat independent adherent who was waiting to see whether the party made good before committing himself definitely.

With Pompey's accession to the consulship the fortunes of the knights, who had suffered untold disasters under Sulla, reached a turning point. The restoration of the censorship meant among other things that the equestrian corporations were again to be assigned provincial contracts; the restoration of the tribuneship meant that they would not have to appeal to the hostile senate for desired administrative measures; the revision of the court panels gave back to them both power and prestige. Since Pompey proved to be their friend they determined to honor him and use him further. In 67 they demanded that the seas be cleared of pirates so that the commerce in which they were interested would be protected; and they demanded that Pompey be placed in command of the war with extraordinary powers. When the senate objected, the knights, resting their arguments upon Gracchan precedents, took the bill directly to the assembly. The senate considered this revolutionary. The populace, flattered by this appeal to their assembly and favorably disposed to Pompey, supported the knights. When the senate induced a tribune to veto the measure, Gabinius, assuming the validity of the Gracchan theory of "recall," threatened to present a bill to depose this tribune, thereby forcing him to desist. This was tantamount to accepting the democratic theory of popular sovereignty in its extreme form, and Cicero seems to have acquiesced. At any rate when Cicero mentioned the incident in the *Pro Cornelio* two years later, he raised no objection to the procedure, and afterwards when he quarreled with Gabinius he did not cast this act in his teeth.

In the year 66, when Manilius introduced a proposal to place Pompey in command in Asia, the same coalition of knights and populace again insulted the senate by taking the bill directly to the assembly. On this occasion Cicero was the principal speaker for the coalition; and he spoke as a full-fledged democrat, unashamed. One may of course suppose that Cicero was largely influenced by life-long connections with the knights and by a deep devotion to Pompey, apparently dating from the time when he served under Pompey's father in the Social War. One also realizes that the Manilian law had a very great practical appeal, and that a rising and ambitious young statesman like Cicero would see the advantage of being chosen as the spokesman for such an important measure of the party then in power. Be that as it may, the speech of that day is the speech of an important and accepted member of the popular-equestrian party.[6]

This was the year of Cicero's praetorship in which he had to serve as judge in the trial of Licinius Macer, a radical democrat, who was accused of misappropriation. Cicero mentions the case to Atticus immediately after the trial, remarking—though a judge had but little discretion in such matters— that he had been favorably disposed to the culprit in his management of the case, and had received much favorable comment from the people for his attitude.[7]

[6] *De Imperio Cn. Pompei.*
[7] *Ad Att.* i. 4; Plut. *Cic.* 9.

A democratic attitude is again shown by Cicero in his defense of Cornelius the next year (65). Cornelius in his tribuneship had angered the senate by proposing several radical plebiscites and especially by his disregard of a tribunician veto. When the herald had been forbidden by a tribune to read the bill of Cornelius in question, Cornelius himself had read it to the assembly, thereby not only breaking an old law but also in a new manner putting into effect the Gracchan theory of the "recall" which would strip the senate of its power to interfere in legislation. When Cornelius was haled to court by some senators on the charge of *lese majesté* Cicero undertook to defend him; in this defense Cicero confined himself to minimizing the charge of the actual breach of a law, but did not offer any apologies for the attempt of Cornelius to apply the radical theory of "recall." Indeed he actually defended that part of the procedure by referring to the precedent set by Gabinius two years before.[8] Here then he accepted again the Gracchan theory of popular sovereignty. In the years 66–5 at least Cicero behaved like a confirmed democrat.

In July of 65, about the time of his speech, Cicero wrote to Atticus that he had begun to think of his canvassing for the consulship and that he was certain of the support of all but the nobles, that is to say, he knew that the equestrian and democratic groups would vote for him. A few days later he still felt himself so closely allied with the democratic group that he was considering giving legal aid to Catiline. That however he did not do. A careful

[8] *Pro Corn.* ed. Stengl. p. 57.

investigation into the merits of the case was probably enough to dissuade him.

This year in fact proved a new turning point in Cicero's politics. Pompey had now been absent for two years and his coalition lacked effective leadership. The democrats had suffered in prestige by electing to the consulship Autronius and Sulla, who were presently convicted of bribery and deposed. In the reaction against the radicals two conservatives had been elected. The deposed candidates made matters worse for their party by entering into (or so it was widely rumored) a conspiracy to seize power, only to fail again. Catiline, one of their aides, continued the agitation with more and more questionable proposals, and the party was so far discredited that the soberer element began to look for saner leadership. The party itself, under such leadership as Catiline could give, drifted far toward the left, and among the stronger men only ambitious politicians like Caesar and Crassus—who hoped to use its fortunes to their advantage—remained in nominal allegiance. Cicero of course could not follow such guidance, and it is probable that most of the property-owning knights had drifted rightward before the year was over. These men of the middle class had been willing to support the Gracchan theory of popular sovereignty because it seemed to insure the possibility of progressive legislation; but when the more radical democrats began to talk of using the assembly for monetary inflation and moratoria on private debts, the knights were of course frightened. Caesar and Crassus added to their fears by proposing to ask for imperialistic commands for themselves and to check the power of Pompey who had been winning provinces which the knights hoped to exploit under a stable régime. Unfortunately none of Cicero's utterances have survived from this momentous year (July 65 to July 64) when, like the rest of the knights, he must have drifted steadily away from the old coalition, or rather when he saw the left wing of the party drifting steadily away from the time-honored Roman devotion to law and property rights.

Before the election of 64, in which Cicero stood for the consulship, Catiline became ever more a demagogue and made an alliance with the unprincipled Antonius. These two men received the support of Caesar and Crassus, but of course not of the moderates. The conservative element of the state disliked to vote for a *novus homo* like Cicero, but the only other sound candidates were Cornificius and Galba, who were little known and fairly sure of defeat. Cicero was certain to get most of the equestrian vote, he would draw heavily from the popular vote because of his well-known liberal connections, he had the favor of Pompeian soldiers and adherents, and on economic and social questions he could be trusted. The optimates therefore decided to support him although he was not one of them. But the veering was not all on their part. Cicero also had learned from the talk of Catiline, Caesar, and Crassus that the Gracchan theory of popular sovereignty without a senatorial check might lead to dangerous economic and imperialistic legislation. He accordingly abandoned the theory that the senate had no constitutional right to inter-

fere in the popular will, a theory which he had supported in 66 and 65. He doubtless said so in the
senate before election day, when saying so would
count. At any rate very soon after he assumed office,
when the question of the senate's *auctoritas* came up
in Caesar's prosecution of Rabirius, he threw all his
energy into the defense of Rabirius and the senate's
right to proclaim martial law,[9] and he did so by
reminding the people that their great leader Marius,
contrary to his party politics, had recognized the
authority of the senate when a great crisis came.
This served well as an apology, if one were needed,
for his own abandonment of the central democratic
doctrine when his eyes had been opened to its dangers. Cicero thus led the knights into a coalition
with the optimates and continued through the year
to cement a *concordia ordinum*.

During the summer the second violent canvass
of Catiline on a reckless program of revolution only
made Cicero a more confirmed conservative. To
save the state from revolution he had himself to
propose a senatorial order of martial law in October,
a measure he would doubtless have fought three
years before, and under its provisions he had the
conspirators put to death, an act which made him
the prime defender and advocate of the central
optimate theory, and later caused his banishment
at the hands of Caesar's democratic coalition. Thus
experience and circumstances had in three years

[9] Hardy (*Jour. Phil.* XXXIV, 16) denies that the question of the
senate's *auctoritas* was at stake in this trial, since Sallust's *Catiline* and
Caesar's *Bell. Civ.* admit the constitutionality of the *Sen. Cons. Ult.*
But Sallust and Caesar wrote almost twenty years later, after Caesar
had packed the senate for use in any measure he chose. The question
was then no longer of any importance. Cicero's speech, *Pro Rabirio*,
definitely says that the issue at stake was the senate's authority.

turned the avowed democrat into an extreme optimate. It is needless to follow his career in detail:
the desertion of his coalition by the knights because
Caesar offered them what they desired, his banishment, which only confirmed his convictions that he
was right, his failure on his return to undo Caesar's
popular legislation because the senate feared Caesar
and dared not follow Cicero. He still clung for a
while to his new doctrine of the senate's importance,
as the *Pro Sestio* proves, but it was a futile policy.
The senators, fearing Caesar, failed to respond. He
saw then, if not before, that the senate could not
rule Rome.

Cicero now retired from active political life and
found time to think and draw conclusions from his
experiences for a carefully considered review of
Roman political needs. In the *De Republica*, which
he wrote in 54–1, shortly before the Civil War, he
carefully reviewed the history of the Roman constitution in order to lay a sound foundation for a dur-
able and reasonable program in case the senate and
people should ever regain the freedom of action
which the first "triumvirate" had taken away.
There was some hope that such a program might
have a chance, for Crassus was out of reach and
Pompey and Caesar were noticeably falling apart.
In this book he shows that Rome had definitely
rejected autocratic government, and that, as Polybius had already seen, it had combined the machinery
of popular sovereignty with aristocratic checks under
strong but short-term executives. In showing that
this form was historically based and that it had
operated well in the happiest days of Rome, Cicero

became convinced that he must give a larger place in his book to the popular assembly than he had been willing to accord it since the days of Catiline. He says with rather surprising firmness that the populace must have liberty of action or they will revolt, and that liberty was a natural right that no man of intelligence could propose to destroy. This is virtually a confession that he had gone too far toward oligarchy in his own consulship. He knew now that if the nobles had been more friendly to the populace, Caesar would not have been able to seize control. He therefore admits the theory of popular sovereignty which could not be denied after the events of 59, but he also seeks for some method by which to check the danger of such a concession. His new theory is that the body politic should be educated to accept the leadership and advice of some strong person who might, like the revered *princeps senatus* of old, be honored as guardian (*rector* or *gubernator*) and whose considered advice would be respected by all. He says explicitly that he has in mind such a man as Scipio Aemilianus, who at times served in just such a capacity even when he held only the honorary designation of *princeps senatus*.

In the fragments that we have the precise intention of the great office does not come out clearly. One scholar believes that Cicero had Pompey in mind, and that Augustus later tried to put the program in action under his own régime.[10] A few years later Cicero in a letter to his most trusted

[10] E. Meyer, *Caesars Monarchie:* a thesis questioned by Heinze. Sabine and Smith, *Cicero on the Commonwealth* (1929), keep their attention too closely to the Greek sources.

friend says that Pompey had never measured up to the height of his ideal rector,[11] which seems to be a confession that Cicero had had Pompey in mind as a possible candidate though fearing that Pompey would prove deficient as a leader. It can hardly be doubted that Cicero must have had moments of regrets that the state had not accepted him, Cicero, for such unofficial leadership after his consulship. It is quite clear that if Cicero had at that time proved himself a man of outstanding qualities of leadership he might have become for many years a rector of the type that he describes. At any rate in 43, after Caesar's murder, Cicero assumed for himself the position of rector and gubernator, though he held no office.[12] However, while writing the *De Republica* in 54–1, Cicero could hardly have supposed that his day of influence would return so long as Caesar or Pompey continued in power.

Another possibility is that when Caesar appeared to be aiming at some form of autocracy, Cicero entertained the hope of converting that powerful man by his monograph on government to accept a constitution of good old traditions and to assume under that constitution a legal and dignified position such as Scipio had for a while enjoyed. There is at any rate a significant passage in the *De Provinciis Consularibus*,[13] written in the year 56 (two years before he began to write the *De Republica*) in which, after much flattering of Caesar, he suggested

[11] *Ad. Att.* viii. 11.

[12] He does, however, not use those terms: cf. *Fam.* xi. 6: *adpetam huius rei principatum; Fam.* xii, 24, 2 (Jan. 43): *me principem senatui populoque Romano professus sum; Fam.* x. 28: *totam rem publicam sum amplexus.*

[13] *De Prov. Proc.* 38 ff.

that since Caesar was as moderate as he was wise he would be willing to accept a constitutional position and act in harmony with the senate, if the senate would act in a conciliatory manner. That passage may be the safest clue to follow in trying to fathom the intentions of the *De Republica*.

Cicero's hopes, however, were shattered. Pompey continued to fall short of deserving full confidence, and Caesar grew into a politician bent on his own advancement. The civil war and the victory of Caesar antiquated the doctrine that Cicero had preached in the *De Republica*, and he had to revise his program once more. Caesar's dictatorship temporarily destroyed the republic, but Cicero could not avoid hoping that there might be a day of recovery. When he wrote the *De Legibus*[14] a few years later, Pompey was dead, Caesar was playing the tyrant and Cicero himself had little hope of gaining the helm of influence. He therefore abandoned the idea of a *rector*, and yet he knew that if Caesar should die or be removed the state would again need a constitution. In this new work accordingly he reverts to the historical tradition of the Scipionic republic, but openly assigns to the senate the leadership that it tacitly had had before Scipio's day, by proposing to allow the senate to control legislation by the requirement of a vote of ratification (*eius decreta rata sunto*). This proposed change, which would eliminate the dangers inherent in the tribunate, shows that Cicero had learned from Caesar's career that a rector might become too

[14] See C. W. Keyes, "Original Elements in Cicero's Ideal Constitution," *Am. Jour. Phil.*, 1921, 309 ff. A part of the *De Leg.* was written before Pompey's death.

powerful, that while popular sovereignty must be recognized as a safety-valve in legislation, the senate must be given a firmer hold on legislation so that it might check both the assembly and the magistrates at critical moments. He was once more, and for reasons easy to comprehend, an advocate of aristocracy.

Cicero had only one brief opportunity to take the helm once more, and then, in the war against Antony, during the last year of his life, the state was in such confusion and under such stress of compulsion that it is not easy to say what theory of the constitution Cicero actually followed. During his unofficial leadership (he probably had frequent occasion to think of himself as the *rector* of his *De Republica*) the senate carried on the war under a *senatus consultum ultimum*, which was regular enough at times of internal disturbance. When it was necessary to impose a direct tax upon all citizens—which had not been necessary since 167—the senate seems to have voted the measure without reference to the assembly. But this also, illogical as it may seem,[15] followed precedent. Finally, it was the senate that annulled the legislation of Antony, for which there was also an abundance of precedents. There was, however, one piece of legislation during this period which betrays the direction of Cicero's thought. The *lex Vibia*,[16] an act to confirm

[15] The senate, though not a representative body, had voted all tax bills before the tribute was abandoned in 167 B.C. There is little doubt that the Gracchi would have altered this illogical procedure if the tribute had remained in their day. In 43 Cicero probably followed the only ancient precedent there was without considerations of political theory.

[16] Cic. *Phil.* x. 17: *legem comitiis centuriatis ex auctoritate nostra laturus est* (Vibius Pansa).

the legality of Caesar's deed, was ordered to be submitted to the *centuriate assembly* on an *auctoritas senatus*, and this shows clearly that the democratic constitution of Caesar's régime was now out of favor. The plebeian assembly could hardly have been slighted in this instance through fear of the lower classes, for the measure was popular enough. It was clearly a procedure which could only have meant that Cicero intended the senate to control legislation by use of the most conservative machinery provided by the old constitution of Rome. Cicero's last acts therefore reveal him even farther away from the democratic policy than those of his consulship.

This review reveals Cicero as inconsistent in party loyalty; it shows that he began as a moderate, then, forced by hatred of Sullan tyranny and induced by immediate practical needs, that he plunged well into democracy, only to be driven by the democratic excesses and the offices of responsibility deeply into conservative sympathies. Experience and observation next led him to revise his theories, first in the direction of liberalism, then, reacting to Caesar's errors, toward conservatism. Yet we need not, with Mommsen, call Cicero a turncoat. He generally followed a straighter course than the parties that shifted all about him. Nor need we, with Heinze, insist that he was consistently an optimate all the years before his consulship, for he was always willing to seek new theories of government when experience proved the old ones inadequate. Finally, Zielinski's view that he acted generally on theories found in his reading is perhaps less justified than any other. Cicero read widely and certainly gained some of his ideas from books—the source-hunter may find parallels in abundance—but when Cicero acted it was not merely because of what he had found in a book, but because he had had actual experience and was feeling his way to the logical conclusion of his observations.

Here we have attempted to illustrate very briefly how Cicero reached his conclusions in political theory through experience, as in a preceding chapter we stressed forensic experience as the chief formative factor of Ciceronian prose. In both of these fields Cicero wrote not primarily as a well-read man transmitting the views of others, but rather as the chief authority of his day by virtue of his own accomplishments. In tracing the body of philosophic essays which he compiled with amazing speed during the six months of retirement in the year 45, we find a very different product, for, as he told Atticus, who was surprised by this prolific output, these are and purport to be merely paraphrases and translations from the Greek.

In a sense, of course, we find the fruit of Cicero's experiences in these also, since he usually chose for paraphrasing what he felt to be significant, and in each work he omitted what met with his disfavor, expanding and illustrating the ideas which appealed to him. Furthermore, since he was concerned rather in presenting clearly the points that interested him than in giving a faithful translation of the Greek, the resultant essays often, even when they are to some extent mosaics, give us very precisely the Ciceronian pattern. Large parts of his philosophical compilations may therefore be taken to illustrate Cicero's own convictions reached through his own experience; and when we deal with such work it may be more fruitful to consider Cicero's own contribution to the final design than to hunt the original quarry from which he drew each *tessera*.

Let us turn to another illustration of how Cicero's views altered and enlarged through personal experience until at last, even though he expressed himself through paraphrased passages, he succeeds in making us feel that he is giving us an epitome of his own personal convictions. For this purpose we may consider his statements about the survival of the soul after death.

In his youth, especially during the civil wars when a public career seemed for a time closed, Cicero had devoted much time to the study of philosophy, and, being a normal Roman of the old type, to whom the actualities of life meant more than metaphysical speculation, for whom the world of realities was too full of interest to allow any time for mystical contemplation, he had naturally accepted the agnostic attitude of the New Academy toward the "unknowable." With the New Academy he was theoretically ready to admit "probabilities," even to act on probabilities, but epistemology had no appeal for him. Of course there are degrees of likelihood and the degrees are apt to vary with mood and occasion. When Cicero spoke before the populace he could see enough plausibility in the argument for Divinity to assume its existence for the time being. But when he wrote to his intimate friends the likelihood did not seem pressing enough to receive mention. He supposed with many other agnostic statesmen of his day that official worship of the gods was useful in the maintenance of the social system,[17] and this explains why, when he stood before the people, giving official advice, his faith seemed to expand. We need not take such faith very seriously. With the problem of the survival of the soul—except for a brief toying with a Platonic Myth in the *De Republica*—Cicero did not concern himself till very late in life. Like most Romans he explained to himself the phrases of the Greek mystics in a simple formula of "Gloria," which, when analyzed, resolved itself into something like the "immortality of fame."[18]

We all know how great a rôle the insistence upon fame and reputation played in the education of the aristocracy at Rome. Since parents and teachers had no religious authority and no fixed ethical sanctions to which to appeal in presenting the claims of duty, the examples of ancestral heroes and the *mos majorum* came to be their decalogue. In their own homes children were shown the *imagines* of their famous ancestors and taught to read the inscribed *tituli* of their honors and triumphs. "Go thou and do likewise" was the obvious inference from daily lessons. It is safe to say that the constantly instilled respect for heroic ancestors was the most powerful factor in ethical teaching that ancient Rome knew. When Cicero so readily drops into the remark that what concerns him is what posterity

[17] *De Natura Deor.* i. 3, written during the summer of 45.

[18] On Cicero's use of Gloria see *Pro Rabirio*, 29–30; *Pro Archia*, 28; *Pro Sestio*, 47; *Ad Att.* ii, 5. Late in life Cicero wrote a treatise in two books on this subject.

will say of him a thousand years hence, he reveals the effectiveness of this moral pedagogy. Again and again in his speeches he frankly admits that *Gloria*, the immortality of fame, is what spurs him to incessant activity. The immortality of the "Choir Invisible"[19] was the only survival that the normal Roman of the cultured classes of the time expected.

Cicero, who read very widely in Greek writers, had of course come in contact with many mystics. He had enjoyed the poetry of Plato's myths; he was a good friend of Neo-Pythagoreans like Nigidius Figulus, with whom he had long conversations on this very subject at Ephesus in 51; he had also conversed with and read the works of Posidonius, who interpolated much oriental mysticism into his Stoicism. But all of this had left few traces in Cicero's utterances, until a very great grief overwhelmed him.[20] In February of the year 45, two years before his death, his daughter Tullia, his one deep passion, died after years of suffering. Cicero gave in completely to his sorrow and withdrew to the forest of Astura, where he walked alone and communed with himself for several weeks. All his friends sent him letters of consolation, but they were typical Roman letters that gave little cheer, only reminding him that it was the duty of a Cicero to be strong, that life had little of value now that liberty was lost, that his own life was near its end. What he wanted was some ray of hope, and he sought the books of the mystics to give him what he needed. He read

[19] George Eliot used as a motto for her poem on this theme the very words of Cicero written when he proposed to erect the shrine to Tullia: *longumque illud tempus cum non ero, Att.* xii. 18.

[20] Warde Fowler, *Religious Experience*, 385, has seen the significance of this experience.

and pondered and temporarily accepted a "probability" that he had occasionally used in speeches to the populace, but never considered of use to himself. And he wrote it out in a *Consolatio* in order to make it more persuasive. The basis of this pamphlet was Crantor's argument, taken from Plato, that the soul reveals capacities that imply eternal existence.[21] But Cicero carried the argument to a conclusion that neither Crantor nor Plato would have accepted, the conclusion that Tullia still lived, would live eternally as a divine being, and if divine must have a shrine. This means that Cicero's new faith, though suggested by reading which had hitherto had no appeal for him, was vitalized now through his deep love for Tullia, that it took its meaning from his own experience, and must reach the conclusion that his love for her dictated. We know, of course, that he sought justification for this conclusion in whatever authority he could find. He says so explicitly in a letter to Atticus:[22]

In trying to escape from the painful sting of recollection I take refuge in recalling something to your memory. Whatever you think of it, please pardon me. The fact is *I find that some of the authors over whom I am poring consider appropriate the very thing that I have often discussed with you, and I hope you approve of it. I mean the shrine.* Please give it all the attention your affection for me dictates. . . . . I shall use all the opportunities permitted in an age as erudite as this to consecrate her memory by every kind of memorial borrowed from the genius of all the masters, Greek and Latin. Perhaps it will only gall my wound: but I consider myself pledged

[21] He quotes it in the Tusculans, i, 68.

[22] *Ad. Att.* xii. 18; it is curious that in this very letter he still reverts when speaking of himself, to his old agnosticism in longum illud tempus *cum non ero.*

by a kind of vow or promise; and I am more concerned
about the long ages when I shall not be than about my
short day, which, short though it is, seems all too long
to me. I have tried everything and find nothing that
gives me rest.

In Greek writers, who justified the apotheosis of
Hellenic rulers by appealing to the cult of "Heroes,"
he could find such arguments and he seems even to
have employed Euhemeristic writings, for he ended
the strange *Consolatio* with the words:[23]

If the children of Cadmos, of Amphion and of Tyndarus were carried to heaven in glory, she too deserves
this honor. This I shall accomplish and with the approval
of the immortal gods shall declare and consecrate you
before all the world....as one of the immortals.

His well-stocked library of Greek books was full of
such mystical ideas, but they had had no meaning
for him till this moment. Now he seized the idea
with determination, and to Atticus, who doubtless
thought it a passing whim and gave him no encour-
agement, he wrote almost every day urging him to
find a suitable spot for the shrine he proposed to
consecrate, and to engage an architect who should
plan its erection.

This mood of mysticism probably lasted only a
few months. The reading he went through in seeking
justification for his conclusions led him to write the
Hortensius, that enthusiastic eulogy of philosophy
which converted St. Augustine to a new mode of life.
In its fragments we find traces of the same un-Roman
mysticism. Then in the first *Tusculan Disputation*,
which he wrote in May of the same year, he repeated
the gist of the argument which he had used in the

[23] Quoted by Lactantius, *Inst. Div.* i, 16.

Consolatio and with nearly as much assurance. However, in this same month he began his first draft of the *Academica*, a careful review of epistemological theory, and this brought him back to his earlier agnosticism. His letters now show less interest in the proposed shrine. In July they cease entirely: it would seem that the "apotheosis" of Tullia was abandoned.

Let us take one more illustration. James Bryce once reckoned that Roman law was still influential in the courts of about three hundred million people; and he pointed out that it had gained this capacity because the jurists of the Empire had based every paragraph of the statutes upon the general principle of equity. Stroux, in his brilliant monograph entitled *Summum jus summa injuria*, has recently demonstrated that Cicero, employing Aristotelian rules of rhetoric, exerted a powerful influence upon the reform of Roman Law by emphasizing in his rhetorical treatises the claims of equity as against statute, and of intention (*voluntas*) as against the literal interpretation of the word. This is all to the good. But the process was hardly as simple as that. The Aristotelian rules of rhetoric had worked no vast reforms in Greece, and at Rome they were not likely to prove less arid in practical life if left to the mercy of text-books. Ideas do not readily revive in that impersonal fashion.

There are two very definite reasons why the ideas of equity and intention had a fair chance to grow into importance in the Ciceronian court. The first is the existence of the peregrine court. As early as 242 B.C. the senate had created a special court for strangers to use in their litigation with Romans. This was, of course, devised in order to attract traders to Rome with a guaranty that they would be dealt with fairly, and it could only be a tribunal of arbitration seeking to reach equitable decisions regardless of Roman statute and by formulary procedure. We know how this court familiarized the Romans with the standard practices of commercial peoples, how it created a respect for *jus gentium*, how in time it accustomed the Romans to respect equity as a thing more sacred than local law and how it trained them to use the formula, until, by about 150 B.C., even the urban court could abandon the rigid *legis actiones* in favor of the formulary procedure, and the praetor's edict was given standing by the side of statute. It is, of course, inconceivable that phrases advocating a free interpretation of law, translated from rhetorical school books, could have won any response at Rome unless the courts had been ready for them.

But there is another item in the reckoning. Cicero, who studied law at the time when this revolution was taking place in the native courts, set out on a long and influential career of forty years as a lawyer for the defense. In that career he had a greater need than anyone else for what we may call the humane and sociological interpretation of law. He seized, of course, with eagerness upon the rhetorical distinction, provided by the Greeks, between the word and the spirit, between law and equity, but this distinction had already been recognized at Rome by the creation of the peregrine court, had in fact been latent in the long series of laws that brought the plebeians their rights during the several centuries of bloodless compromises of the early Republic. Indeed it is safe to say that Cicero without the aid of alien ideas would necessarily have evolved his enthusiasm for equitable interpretation during his long career as a defensive advocate, using as his tool the Roman court with its formulary procedure, its *jus honorarium*, and its respect for *aequitas* and *jus gentium*.[24] In a word, a reform already in progress at home gave Cicero an excellent opportunity to develop his legal practice on the principles of a liberal interpretation of law and to draw upon Greek authors for useful support for his contention, and thus aid in formulating general principles that made the civil law the text-book of the world.

Cicero was a wide reader, and he appropriated ideas from far and near, but he appropriated and applied what he read at the points where he was doing his own thinking, and he applied it creatively. Such was, throughout his life, Cicero's response to experience.

[24] For Cicero's attitude on *Jus gentium*, see *De Off.* iii. 17; i. 23.

CHAPTER VIII

LUCRETIUS AND HIS READERS

In the third century B.C. we find evidence that some of the Romans had begun to doubt the current religious beliefs. During the Second Punic War, the exaggerated superstition among the lower classes, induced apparently by a series of military disasters, led to a pronounced revolt against religion among the more enlightened element.[1] Ennius, though he reveals a strain of Pythagorean mysticism, natural enough in one educated at Tarentum, aided this movement by translating Euhemerus, whose work seems to have been a utopian romance that incidentally interpreted the gods of Greek myths as human beings honored after death. If we may judge from later quotations from this work it was the incidental element which especially attracted the attention of the Romans. Of course, the Euripidean plays presented by Ennius and Pacuvius familiarized the audiences with the phrases of skepticism, and some of the later Greek comedies, written when faith in the Olympians had virtually gone, were shockingly disrespectful of religion. The *Amphitruo* of Plautus is a case in point. It could hardly have been produced except in Greek dress, but for all that such plays tended to undermine

[1] W. Warde Fowler, *Religious Experience*, chap. XV.

respect for the state cults. The actor's garb was, to be sure, Greek, but the deity ridiculed was called by his Latin name, Jupiter, not Zeus.

Unfortunately a satisfying philosophy did not emerge to take the place of the departing devotion—which though of no great moral worth had possessed a certain constraining influence. The soundest Greek philosophy was itself out of date at home and was nowhere taught abroad. Plato's great faith in ratiocination had created a highly imaged idealism of exceedingly great beauty—moral as well as aesthetic. But it had not withstood the prying curiosity of his sophisticated Greek pupils. Aristotle, afraid of the imagination, had set out almost at once to build science upon a foundation of careful and minute observation before trusting to imagination again. Epicurus, without sufficient equipment in science but stirred by a healthy respect for nature, had evolved a materialistic system on the theories of Democritus and Leucippus, which assumed an evolutionary process of creation without divine intervention. The system was attractive, but so full of inconsistencies and untested hypotheses that it led the shrewder young men of Athens into complete agnosticism. Those who were inclined to mysticism took refuge in Zeno's equally facile pantheism. By the time the Romans were ready to delve into metaphysics, the logical flaws in all systems had been pointed out by the Greeks themselves. The world of thought was in confusion. Men had lost faith in their power to solve the riddle of the universe. Professional philosophers were quarrelling, and the rest were turning away in dismay to nearer tasks.

Rome's introduction to Greek philosophy came at this unhappy moment, and through the tutelage of the most pitiful representatives of Greek metaphysical eristic, which had nothing of value to offer to Rome. In the year 155 Carneades, while serving on an Athenian embassy at Rome, gave a demonstration of his dialectic ability by lauding justice one day and the next proving with equal facility the futility of the preceding speech. The third book of Cicero's *De Republica*, has preserved the gist of his argument. Young men were delighted with the show, but the aged shook their heads. The pragmatist argument seemed to them a dangerous introduction to ethics. Carneades, being a state envoy, must be respected, but Cato insisted that the senate finish its business with him speedily so that he might the sooner be sent home; and when during the next year two Epicurean teachers came to Rome to display their doctrines, the authorities ordered them to leave.[2] Roman cultural history might have been very different if the first philosophers had come with a positive message, if the Platonic dialogues had still been in vogue, or if the minds of the slow-moving Romans had been gradually prepared for the incoming skepticism by proofs that this new philosophy was itself but a transient phase. As it was, the leap from old-time orthodoxy to untrammeled agnosticism was too great. The danger to political and civic stability was fully sensed by the cautious senators. The demonstration of the ridiculous futility of the new learning, if culture produced men like these prattling Greeks, was all too patent. Rome was projected into a fear

[2] *Athenaeus* xii. 68.

and hatred of metaphysical dialectic that a century of similar experiences hardly removed. Only Panaetius, the Stoic, had better success, for, concerning himself less with metaphysics, giving more attention to ethics of a type that justified Roman ideas of jurisprudence and political activity, he was welcomed by the small circle of men who acknowledged the leadership of the younger Scipio. Stoicism thus gained respectability, but it was Stoicism prudently narrowed to ethical dogmatism.

After a generation or two of hesitation young men of family began to attend lectures in Athens. They were almost all sons of senators who were themselves preparing for public life, and they chose their teachers and courses accordingly. They needed familiarity with Greek not only because of its great literature but because Greek was the language of a very important part of the now expanding empire. They sought tuition especially with the rhetoricians who taught the art of Demosthenes, the art of public address and debate—all-important in the senate and the courts. What system of philosophy students happened to imbibe was determined by this fact, since the professors of philosophy were the heads of the scholastic hierarchies and each style of speech had a direct connection with an appropriate school of philosophy. It was not accidental that the young man who preferred a matter-of-fact style found himself also imbibing stoic philosophy, and that the one who desired a more florid manner got his philosophic needs satisfied in the circles of the New Academy. This union of rhetoric and philosophy will in part explain why Epicurean materialism was somewhat slow to reach the attention of the Romans, since the school of Epicurus gave little time to rhetoric and therefore caught few of the young men who were training for statesmanship. Furthermore, it is not difficult to comprehend why in these circumstances and in view of the fact that philosophy was no longer progressive or fruitful it continued to remain a matter of minor importance at Rome. Rome's young nobles were going to Athens for political training, not for a general education, and their teachers accordingly gave out their philosophical lectures as ancillary to rhetorical studies.

So much must be kept in mind by way of an introduction to the work of Lucretius, the friend of Cicero, who was the first of the Romans to present a philosophic theme in an attractive literary garb. In speaking of him here we shall not be primarily concerned with Lucretius as a poet, for the art of Lucretius springs out of an inspiration not to be explained by sources or environment, nor shall we speak primarily of the philosophical system of the *De Rerum Natura*—for he invents his philosophy as little or as much as did Milton or Tennyson or Browning their theology or their social philosophy. We wish rather to dwell upon Lucretius in his Roman setting, his response to it, and its effects upon him.

Of Lucretius himself we know very little, and that we owe chiefly to a few strange remarks of St. Jerome, who disliked materialism as did all the fathers of the church. The dates are probably 99–55

B.C. If so Lucretius was slightly younger than Caesar and died eleven years before Caesar's assassination. He was old enough to have observed with full comprehension all the wretched cruelty of the civil wars between the Marian and Sullan factions, and that would have been enough to turn a sensitive man away from political life. Lucretius speaks repeatedly of Latin as *patria lingua* which implies that Rome was the native city of his family, and he also reveals a certain Roman pride in his reference to foreigners as well as a sympathy with the aristocracy in his slighting references to the crowd.[3] The life of Rome was familiar to him. His name was well known from the day of Lucretia, the insult to whose honor had stirred the riots which led to the expulsion of the tyrant Tarquin. At least thirty-six men bore the name with sufficient distinction to earn space in the modern classical encyclopedia. But whether the poet belonged to one of the nobler branches of the family we do not know. If, as is quite possible, he was a son of the general who was murdered by Sulla because of his independence we would comprehend his horror of warfare. His cognomen, Carus, is somewhat less usual in early records than his nomen, but it was in good standing from its first occurrence some two centuries before the poet's time till late in the Empire.[4] From the manner in which Lucretius addresses Memmius, a man of some family and distinction, Munro reasonably assumed

[3] *Patria*, iii. 260; iv. 970; i. 41. See the introduction of Merrill's excellent edition of Lucretius, pp. 13–14.

[4] Marx was of course in error in stating that the name Carus implied humble ancestry. See "The Name T. Lucretius Carus," in *Studies in Honor of Hermann Collitz* (1930); p. 63.

that the poet was on a footing of equality with this member of the minor nobility.

Lucretius' great poem, *On Nature*, was apparently being written during the middle decade of the last pre-Christian century. It was not quite complete when the poet died; the preface addresses Memmius as one who is in the midst of danger and apparently in arms,[5] a reference perhaps to Memmius' governorship of Bithynia in 57. But the preface assumes the present arrangement of books, which was not established till books 1, 2 and 4 had been written. Perhaps this foreword was thrown in for an incomplete presentation copy to accompany Memmius when he sailed to Bithynia in the spring of 57. Of the legend that the poet experienced intervals of insanity I need only repeat the judgment of the noted physician Dr. Osler:[6] "Of love-philtres that produce insanity we may read the truth in a chapter of that most pleasant manual of erotology, the *Anatomy of Melancholy*. Of insanity of any type that leaves a mind capable in lucid intervals of writing such verses as *De Rerum Natura* we know nothing. The sole value of the myth is its casual association with the poem of Tennyson." This of course does not preclude the possibility that Lucretius committed suicide in a fit of madness, though what a father of the church reports about a member of the Epicurean sect must not be taken too seriously. Wishful thinking often ends in the misjudging of sources.

[5] See *Class. Phil.* XIV, 286.

[6] Dr. Osler's Presidential Address to the Classical Association (England), 1918–19.

The poem of Lucretius may be classed with Milton's *Paradise Lost* as a purposive work of art. Milton set out to "justify the ways of God to man" in verses that should carry the reader by their sheer emotional beauty; Lucretius, while equally aware of the demands of art, proclaimed his chief purpose to be to remove fear of the gods by describing creation as natural and independent of divine intervention. Milton is one of the last of the didactic poets; Lucretius wrote while the didactic tradition was still generally accepted. He wrote in verse because his predecessors, the earlier philosophers had done so, had indeed composed wholly in verse at a time when reading and writing were not general, when teaching was by word of mouth, and rhythm seemed a legitimate aid to memory. Didactic verse, at first a necessity, had established itself by its very bulk, and was accepted as a customary form by Ennius and Vergil as well as by Lucretius. The effort that the modern reader finds in adapting himself to imaginative and highly colored phraseology employed in scientific arguments need not be strenuous if one accepts the tradition as then vital and unquestioned.

Lucretius' argument in briefest form is this: Crimes that disturb society are due to fear—fear of death. This fear grows out of an apprehension of what the gods may do to one's erring soul. The desire to avoid death and the dreaded hereafter drives men to accumulate wealth and power by evil means. Obviously the way to reach a life of peace, is to believe that death is simple dissolution and that the gods are not concerned in the least about human behavior. The proof that this belief is well founded lies in the atomistic philosophy of Epicurus, which explains the creation of the universe from a concourse of atoms, without divine activity, and considers living things, including man, as atomic, and which interprets human progress not in terms of divine interference but in terms of a theory of the "survival of the fittest." Such is Lucretius' argument. It is full of fallacies, as science has always been. Our generation was brought up on Dalton's solid, immaterial molecule which now seems as antiquated as the Lucretian atom. The Curies shattered that, and we accepted in its place the electron of Rutherford; then five years ago the Quantum theory led to Bohr's kaleidoscopic atom which has since given way to the new theories of Schrödinger and those who vigorously question the material atom. In 1907 Ostwald called the law of conservation the greatest discovery of the nineteenth century, but by 1924 scientists doubted whether it was a law at all. That has happened in one brief lifetime. We do not ask for finality in science, though like Lucretius the young scientist of each new generation seizes upon the latest hypothesis and assumes it to be true. The theory of electrons, whether right or wrong, seems to some of us to have justified itself not only because of its power to awaken the imagination, but in its capacity as a solvent that could disintegrate preceding dogmatism by seeming to prove itself more efficacious. Such was the beauty which Lucretius discovered in his new-found science. To him personally it meant release, romance, and poetry, and he spent all his energy trying to give to others what he had found. He assures us that his whole being is pierced with a thrill when he lets his mental eye see the vision of creation.

> Moenia mundi
> discedunt, totum video per inane geri res.

He becomes so absorbed in his work that he sits the night out phrasing what he has beheld, and finally when he drops to sleep his dreams are still of the vision of creation.

At the very outset however, we stumble upon a deep puzzle in attempting to picture the man in his setting. How could he suppose that fear of punishment after death was the determining factor in social ethics, when the Romans of this period had not yet developed any clear eschatological system, and when only the learned had begun to read the Platonic myths and Stoic fancies regarding a possible future life? Cicero in his old age, when after utter defeat and a very deep personal grief he needed faith in a doctrine of compensation, tried to find arguments for a theory of the soul's survival. But the *Tusculans* do not represent Cicero in the heyday of his powers when, like other cultured Romans, he thought of immortality only in terms of surviving fame. Caesar assumed when he spoke in the senate that his audience accepted death as final, and Catullus gave the common view in his *Nox est perpetua una dormienda*. The tombstone inscriptions of the Republican period are quite reticent on the point, whereas the more garrulous ones of the Empire that teem with mystical phraseology belong largely to slaves from Asia. The epitaphs of genuine

Romans are silent about future punishments and rewards.

It does not suffice to say that the central argument of the *De Rerum Natura* comes from Epicurus. The language of Lucretius is so vigorous and goes so much farther than Epicurus that we may be sure that some personal experience inspired it. Now the Etruscans, north of the Tiber, had long ago developed a very definite picture of what life after death was like. The wall-paintings on Etruscan tombs give delightful pictures of the banquets of the blest—but also gruesome portraits of Charon and of Tuchulcha scourging the souls of the damned. Giotto's frescoes and Dante's pictures of the lost souls in hell give almost as true an interpretation of Etruscan as of Christian conceptions. If we had a biography of Lucretius we might perhaps find that he had spent some years of his boyhood among the Etruscans or that he had had an Etruscan nurse who filled him with un-Roman superstitions which only a carefully considered philosophy could dispel. To a poetic imagination as sensitive as his, such childish beliefs might have occasioned moments of excruciating pain. We do not know the explanation. All that I would suggest at this point is that the poet may well have had some experience in his youth which gave a color to the poem that surprises us in a contemporary of Cicero and which made the new Epicurean faith of special value to him.

It is just possible that an incorrect analysis of instincts led him to stress this point. Taking a suggestion of Epicurus that fear is the cause of abnormal behavior, he drove it hard. He seems not to have surmised that fear of death was readily to be explained as an inheritance from those who had most successfully shunned death; instead he sought to explain the instinct for self-preservation by superstition and to blame that superstition for the acts that are in fact induced by a powerful instinct. How he asks, could a man let greed so dominate him that he would steal, deceive, and even murder, unless he were driven by an inordinate desire to escape the want which might bring death and suffering after death? Such is the argument which seems to be largely his own.

In his purpose then, he is wholly sincere, whatever we may think of the logic of his argument. However, he betrays in his enthusiasms the fact that what inspires him is not a negative missionary spirit, but the desire to let every man know the beauty of science. Plato spoke of the hypnotic vision of "ideas"—the ecstatic thrill that came to the philosopher who penetrated into divine knowledge. We know with what enthusiasm Sir Isaac Newton's announcement of the laws of gravitation was greeted, with what joy scientists in our own day heard of the breaking-up of the atom and of the cosmic rays that penetrate our atmosphere. Similar must have been the exaltation of this Roman when he felt that he could lay aside childish superstitions, suddenly pierce the confines of the universe and behold the nebulae shaping into planets, when he realized, as he thought, that energy lived forever, that matter was eternal, that the universe was infinite, that in the survival of the fit there were promises of eternal progress, that law and order ruled the universe.

His ibi me rebus quaedam divina voluptas
percipit atque horror.

It amazed him to find himself so carried away that
he could not sleep, that he must sit the whole night
through satisfying his soul with the vision he had
caught. Materialism has been called an unpoetic
theme. To us it may be, but to a Roman brought
up in the dull mazes of polytheism and the ludicrous
nursery-tales that masqueraded as cosmology, it
was a sudden liberation. He had found a theme of
the highest poetic worth, the epic story of the
origins of life; and Vergil who half rejected his
arguments still was poet enough to see that Lucretius had discovered the sublimest of all poetic
themes—*Felix qui potuit.*

The young men who were growing up when
Lucretius' poem was published turned quickly to
his faith, despite the fact that the Athenian garden
had till then been unpopular. It could hardly have
been the doctrine of hedonism—which Lucretius
almost disregards—that enticed the youth. After
all the hedonistic calculus was as exacting in its
morality as was the stoic argument of obedience to
nature. More probably it was the appeal to the
imagination and the aesthetic vision disclosed by
Lucretius that swept the younger generation of that
time off its feet.

There is another fruitful idea, the idea of progress, which first entered Roman consciousness
through the work of Lucretius. Our modern belief
in mechanistic progress, made into a fetish as it
was after the acceptance of Darwinism, at times
obstructs self-criticism and encourages fatalism to
such an extent that its value as a stimulant may

be almost completely negatived. A generation that could rush thoughtlessly into the most stupidly criminal war of all ages—and still blandly insist that it was the supreme fruit of civilization—has surely been gulled by a fallacious evolutionary *post hoc ergo*. It is a wholesome reminder to us post-Darwinists that the Athenians of Pericles' day had in many respects attained to a creative culture which no nation has since succeeded in reaching. Yet read with a careful attention to all its implications, the evolutionary doctrine of progress is productive of envigorating optimism. Before Lucretius wrote—and the poet himself had not entirely shaken himself free from old beliefs—the Romans looked upon the golden age as past, and they were therefore too much reconciled with the fatalism inherent in the conviction that further deterioration was only to be expected.

The belief in a golden age of the past had come from several sources: from Hesiodic genealogies of gods and "heroes," from an early naïve faith in the actuality of Homeric descriptions, from the tendency of parents to contrast the morals of a new generation with the refurbished and selected memories of their youth, and from the utopian pictures of romances conveniently placed in the far away and long-ago. All these things and others begot the "golden age" of Chronos' day. The Romans had found such tales plausible. They too had a splendid tradition of ancestral heroes who had undoubtedly possessed the sterling qualities of a simple puritan-agrarian primitivism—capacity to endure hardship and pain, family devotion, loyalty, and abstinence—

that later Romans admired but too often missed in contemporary life. In their conquests of the world they had come into contact with many uncivilized peoples and had had occasion to note these very qualities in all unadvanced peoples.[7] They had evidence in the ruins of the decayed villages of Latium that the soil no longer bore the population it once had, and the conclusion was ready at hand, as Lucretius himself points out, that mother earth was not so fruitful as she had been in her youth. Furthermore, when they happened upon the tombs of the prehistoric age,[8] especially the vaults of Etruscan princes, they found in many of them the lavish furniture of gold and silver and bronze-ware that led them to accept the Hesiodic chronology—doubtless based in part on similar observations in Boeotia —of a seeming succession of gold, silver, bronze, and iron periods.

Accordingly, there were reasons enough for accepting the well-known utopian fancies of the Greek poets. Lucretius himself did not wholly free himself of these beliefs. The Ennian portraits of the ancient heroes, and the description of primitive simplicity appealed strongly to him. He did not think that the Romans he had seen in the days of the Sullan massacres and the Catilinarian conspiracy were the moral equals of those of an earlier day. In point of fact they were not. There had been a noticeable decline.

[7] Lucr. v. 17.

[8] Lucr. ii. 1168; v. 800, on the decay of agriculture. Most of the magnificent early tombs excavated during the last century were found already rifled; some of these had evidently been found by the Romans and must have yielded wares as rich as those of the Regolini-Galassi tomb.

Nevertheless, as we have seen, the theory of evolution which he adopted made it possible for him to observe that in some respects civilization had actually meant progress, that in the arts, in the domain of thought, in the institutions of government and law there had been a real advance. In his fifth book[9] he remarks in an intimate note that betrays his own personal observations:

> Wherefore even now some arts are receiving their last polish, some are even in course of growth: just now many improvements have been made in ships; only yesterday musicians have given birth to tuneful melodies; then too this nature or system of things has been discovered lately, and I the very first of all have only now been found able to transfer it into native words.

Lucretius' whole sketch of social evolution (V, 1011, ff.), though replete with regret at the errors committed, reveals a strong conviction that on the whole the trend had been toward betterment, and this view is clearly stated at the end (Munro's translation):

> Ships and tillage, walls, laws, roads, arms, dress and all such like things, all the prizes, all the elegancies too of life without exception, poems, pictures, and the chiselling of fine-wrought statues, all these things *practice*, together with the acquired knowledge of the untiring mind, taught men by slow degrees as they advanced on the way step by step. Thus time by degrees brings each several thing forth before men's eyes, and reason raises it up into the borders of light; for things must be brought to light one after the other and in due order in the different arts, until these have reached their highest point of development.

It is sometimes said that Lucretius did not make the final fruitful deduction that progress might con-

[9] v. 332 ff. (tr. Munro).

tinue in the future—which is the dominant note in modern evolutionary literature. It is true that the poet, whose task was to describe rather than to prophesy, does not emphasize the note of optimism, but when he says explicitly that some of the arts "are even now in the process of growth" he has committed himself to the full theory. And if one is convinced that the creative process has on the whole been one of progress, the rest follows, and the theory of the Social Contract to which Lucretius so fully commits himself rests in a deep faith that the best men have aided and will continue to aid progress by their efforts. Vergil, a close reader of Lucretius, was able in the fourth *Eclogue* to shift the golden age into the future, and in the *Georgics* he reveals the conviction that men have themselves, aware of their needs, improved the arts and crafts. Here we see immediately the consequences of the new evolutionary idea. Cicero also exhibits a practical optimism that is ready to undertake the labor of bettering conditions. While he never explicitly discusses the question he traces in his *Brutus* the evolution of Roman oratory showing its successive improvement, and in the *De Republica* and the *De Legibus*, where he accepts the evolutionary theory of social progress, he asserts again and again that it is the duty of statesmen to contribute their efforts to aid this advance. Finally, Seneca has also caught the full import of the gospel of progress. As a Stoic he should have consistently held to the discouraging theory of cycles. That he did not is doubtless due to his great fondness for Epicurean science.[10]

[10] Seneca, *Epist. Mor.*, 64. 7; 104. 16; *Quaest. Nat.* 1 pref., vii. 25–31.

I respect the discoveries of wise men and do reverence to the inventors.... but let us also act the part of good parents: let us increase the inheritance of these things; let the property go to our successors with some increment. Much still remains to be done and will remain; nor will the man born a thousand years hence lack the opportunity to add to what he has received.

Surely Bury has quite missed the point when he holds that the ancient idea of progress failed to look to the future.

Lucretius also responded to Roman temperamental inclinations when he stressed the importance of observation and inductive logic in philosophy. The Romans of the Republic disliked mysticism and were ripe for a cosmology that substituted sense perception for vague mystery. They were also impatient of abstractions, and made little progress with such deductive sciences as mathematics. Their immense experiences in practical affairs of government had accustomed them to the habit of organizing committees to gather data on which to base charters for cities, treaties with neighbors, and forms of government for provinces. Formal plans shaped on a priori ratiocination they had learned to distrust. They always felt their way slowly through experiments to generalizations. It is characteristic of them that without formulating a general principle of equity they shaped a court of equity for the cases of foreigners a hundred years before they found that they were putting into practice the principles that Greek theory had deduced from philosophy without the ability to realize them in actuality.

Democritus had long ago proposed the hypothesis of natural creation, and Lucretius accepted the theory from Epicurus. What Lucretius himself saw was the need of emphasizing to the Romans the approach by induction from observable data to the theories, and the need of presenting these data in a succession of arresting pictures. In his first book, when arguing that there is no creation by miracle, he leads up to the generalization by a series of carefully established facts that give a sound basis for the final induction:

Plants germinate from seeds, they always require time for growth, they require plant-food and the cultivation of the soil that makes that food available, and they invariably grow into the same species as that of the parent plant.

Beneath every statement of this series there lies a mass of careful observation, tested by what John Stuart Mill calls the method of "agreement and difference," and these valid conclusions are in turn used for the final induction that creation by miracle is unknown. Similarly, in the third book, he demonstrates by use of the same logical process that, since sickness, coma, age, poison, and whatever affects the body, also affect the mind, the mind has actual contact with the body. The standard method of "concomitant variations" is also used frequently as, in the second book, where the argument runs thus: since heavy and light bodies fall more nearly uniformly in thin air than in heavy water they would fall at the same rate of speed in a vacuum. Except in the sixth book, which follows sources closely, Lucretius' wealth of examples seems to come largely from his own store.

In truth, most of Mill's categories of inductive methods are implicit in Lucretius, for the Epicureans were in his day busily defending their use of induction against the attacks of Stoics. The logical treatise of Philodemus,[11] which of course Mill did not know, seems to have been written very shortly after Lucretius' death, and it is not at all improbable that Lucretius had heard the lectures of Philodemus before they were finally given to the public. In those lectures the author dwells much on the validity of carefully chosen analogy, for in the field of the unobservable—in evolutionary cosmology, in atomic theory, and in psychology—metaphor and simile have always been and will always be fruitful tools of science. But Philodemus finally insisted on the necessity of basing all inductions on extremely careful observation, of using only essential similarities and pertinent comparisons, and he implied, even if he did not explicitly state it, that every test of "agreement," "difference," and "residue" is necessary. Of course the Epicureans fell into the fallacies of incomplete data, as all science based upon inductive methods must, and as beginners they were obviously impatient of delay and over-opti-

[11] Philodemus, περὶ σημείων, ed. Gomperz, 1865, with additional readings from the papyrus by Philippson in *Rhein, Mus.* (1909). See Weltring, *Das σημεῖον in der Aristotelischen, Stoischen und Epikureischen Philosophie* (Bonn, 1910). Philodemus anticipated some of the difficulties that later troubled Mill, noticing that in some inductive problems a single observation provided valid conclusions, whereas in others very many were required (Gomperz, 19, 13); he knew that many fallacies were due to the use of insufficient instances (Gomp. 30, 2; 35, 15), that it was well not only to observe nature but to conduct systematic research and to employ the observations of others (Philippson, *loc. cit.*, 13), that the observer must choose essential similarities in using the mode of "agreement" and must exclude conclusions as soon as a refuting instance appeared (Gomp. 13, 1; 17, 30; 20, 32), and he emphasized the need of employing the principle of difference (Gomp. 18, 15; Phil. p. 28). This treatise which probably draws lavishly on Zeno, has not yet been fully restored, and being a defense against Stoic attack it is not to be considered a formal and complete exposition of inductive logic. But in germ it contains most of the essential observations of J. S. Mill.

mistic; but the correct forms of the inductive processes were all in daily use and if Bacon and Mill had known the treatise of Philodemus, which so well explains the picturesque arguments of Lucretius, they would have shown more respect for the "wisest of the ancients."

It is in the service of inductive logic that much of Lucretius' startling imagery is invented. The poetic quality of the book is in no sense "purple-patch" work; it is not an adjunct like the Corinthian columns pasted on Roman concrete walls for ornamental purposes. The pictures will always be found to derive from unusually accurate observations of nature so that they may serve their purpose as the starting points of the induction, or, when induction was impracticable, as a basis for some significant analogue. They are so indelibly presented that the argument which they carry cannot be forgotten. To realize their vital function in the argument one has but to recall a few instances of them: the race-horse leaping forward at the gong, the birds that start singing with the first ray of morning light, the flock of pasturing sheep that from a distance seem not to stir, the particles of dust flitting in a shaft of sunlight, the sudden glory of the dawn, the sea gulls screaming over the white-caps, the cow in the pasture distraught when her calf is taken from her, the fishes swimming about in the yielding water, the gnat that is so light that its weight is not felt, the dog barking at dreams or deceived by an imagined scent. The science is no less precise in such passages because of the vivid naturalism of the descriptions. It is indeed adapted to the Roman mode of thought, for the dry unimaged style of Epicurus, all too readily satisfied with dogmatic abstractions, would have made little impression upon the Romans.

One may wonder why it is that, although Lucretius possessed such a clear conception of the processes and tools of inductive logic, so little time was spent in the laboratory experimentation desiderated by Bacon. Our books of logic often assume that man's processes of thought were recent inventions, as if no one argued deductively till Aristotle, or inductively till Bacon. One might as well assume that no human being used the lens of the eye until some one discovered its existence by dissection. Indeed Nausicaa's remarks to Ulysses are as well packed with the fruits of penetrating reasoning as the pleas of a Philadelphia lawyer, and the paleolithic savages who made stone axes and fire pistons in the primeval forests employed the same forms of logic as the modern chemist in his laboratory. Lévy-Brühl's conclusion that the "prelogical man" lived just beyond protohistory is not very convincing to the classicist. What is sometimes called a history of logic is of course not a history of the acquisition of the logical capacity, but a history of the conscious analyses of the processes that have long been in use.

The early Greek writers naturally struck out toward the great engrossing questions of God and the universe. Here analogy and deduction could get quicker results than induction because the problem lay beyond the reach of direct observation. Furthermore, mathematics could then proceed upon a few seemingly universal maxims that had come to be considered self-evident from ages of human experience. Here all progress happened to lie in the deductive forms of thought. However, when advance stopped in this direction, after making the most rapid progress that the history of science can record, and when *a priori* ratiocination was found to lead no farther, then the atomists began at the bottom again with minute observation and patient induction. They used a laboratory method, though it was not at first necessary to make an artificial laboratory, since nature had provided one near at hand with untold data still unrecorded. What need was there of planting seeds and observing the laws of creation in a garden-box until nature's vast gardens had been studied? The method was just as sound and for the time being far more fertile. It was at this point that Lucretius came into the field. Scientific experimentation indeed had already begun at points where nature did not seem to give sufficiently precise results—one recalls Aristarchus and Archimedes—but it had not proceeded far; not however from lack of scientific curiosity, or from failure to appreciate the value of experiments, but because quicker results were still to be had by exploiting nature's abundant store of data.

The appreciation of induction and the employment of the scientific processes by Lucretius must of course not be overstressed. Some of the large gains of formal logic have never been more highly valued than by him. In Epicurus and his predecessors, for instance, the concept of infinity had been arrived at deductively and skilfully employed in order to provide time, space, and material for the evolutionary assumption. Lucretius fully appreciated the value of that concept, realized indeed that the creative process of natural evolution could not for a moment be assumed, for the amazingly intricate Nature which had to be explained, except on the hypothesis of infinity. And infinity was to him not merely a logical necessity, it was a stimulating concept that lifted the imagination of man into the realms of high poetry:[12]

> For my mind-of-man
> Now seeks the nature of the vast Beyond
> There on the other side, the boundless sum
> Which lies without the ramparts of the world,
> Toward which the spirit longs to peer afar,
> Toward which indeed the swift élan of thought
> Flies unencumbered forth.

It is also characteristic of Lucretius as a Roman that while he accepted a philosophy that made all creation kin—in this respect Lucretius may be considered the founder of philosophic Romanticism—he refused to abandon the classical humanism that insisted upon seeing in man the master of his own destiny. There is no doubt about the strong drift toward romanticism throughout the poem. Man is here inseparable from nature. The fiery temper of a choleric man, like the ferocity of the lion, is traced to the atomic composition of the soul.[13] The cool-tempered ox partakes of elements that predominate in men of prudence, and cowardice in man is explained physically as akin to the trembling of the deer. In all this, man is removed from the pedestal to which idealistic philosophy had elevated him, and by a back door, as it were, brought back again

[12] *Trans.* W. E. Leonard.   [13] iii. 290 ff.

into Pan's forest where in the past humans had played with Satyrs and quadrupeds in the happy days of Mythopoeia. That Lucretius fully comprehended the poetic importance of this scientific kinship of all living things is apparent from his proemium where spring is pictured as the mating season, the season of song and joy, for all creation without distinction:

> Et genus aequoreum, pecudes, pictaeque volucres—
> Amor omnibus idem.

For soon as the vernal aspect of day is disclosed, and the birth-favouring breeze of Favonius unbarred is blowing fresh, first the fowls of the air, O Venus, show signs of thee and thy entering in, thoroughly smitten in heart by thy power. Next the wild herds bound over the glad pastures and swim the rapid rivers: in such wise, each made prisoner by thy charms, follows thee with desire, whither thou goest to lead it on. Yes, throughout seas and mountains and sweeping rivers and leafy homes of birds and grassy plains, striking fond love into the breasts of all thou constrainest them each after its kind to continue their races with desire.

Here first in literature we get, emerging out of atomic science, the spring poetry of Troubadour song. Lucretius drew out of his science the full value of Romantic poetry.

But when he had done that he did not forget that he was a genuine Roman and that man must be accorded the dignity due his commanding independence. At this point he took full advantage of the Epicurean *clinamen* and asserted man's power of self-mastery. In the finest soul-atom lies the germ of a free-will. "Whence I ask, has been wrested from the fates the power by which we go forward whither the will leads each?" And even after explaining temperament by reference to atomic make-up, he hastened to qualify his statement by adding: "traces of the different natures left behind, which reason is unable to expel from us, are so exceedingly slight that there is nothing to hinder us from living a life worthy of the gods." Indeed his whole life-work was a mission that revealed him a thorough humanist. The man who devoted his days and nights to expel from society the palsy due to superstition, to induce men to use reason in order that they might gain a "life worthy of the gods" was not devoted to naturism in the modern sense of the word. Indeed in some passages Lucretius seems willing to accept human nature at a very high valuation. The ugliness of life is not primarily due to its flaws, but to nature perverted by imposed fears, unreasoned desires, and artificial institutions that enlightened reason might readily dispose of.[14] There is of course in all this some inconsistency, for there lies lurking beneath it all the age-long battle between Determinism and Freedom, and the inconsistency is made the more apparent because, curiously enough, in Lucretius the poet supports the scientist against the humanist. But when one has finished the poem one leaves it with the conviction that, while the poet has not been repressed, the Roman who was conscious of his moral responsibility has held the pen. In that respect the atomic theories of recent years have not demonstrated that Lucretius was in error.

[14] ii. 23; iii. 57; v. 1105.